A cry for help sho[illegible] Inbox:*

"...I have chronic, immediate pain from using my mouse.

"I don't know what to do and I can't find anyone who truly knows what they're doing as far as setting up a desk/mouse so I don't have perpetual pain."

"Any help would be greatly appreciated."

*Taken verbatim from actual events (The Story of Ellie Bea, p. 275)

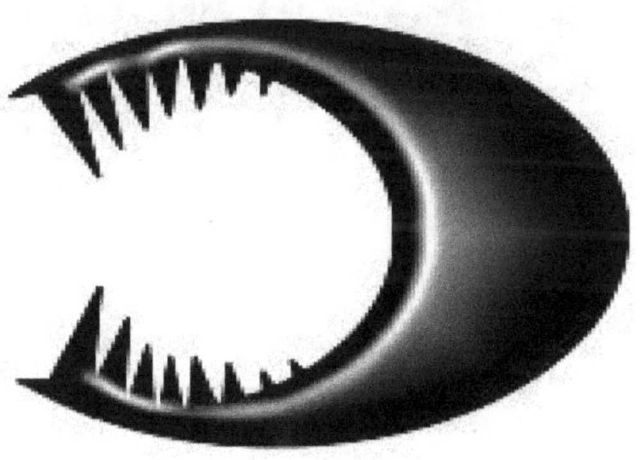

Meet a deadly ethereal predator called BYTR, living inside computer devices, causing her pain.

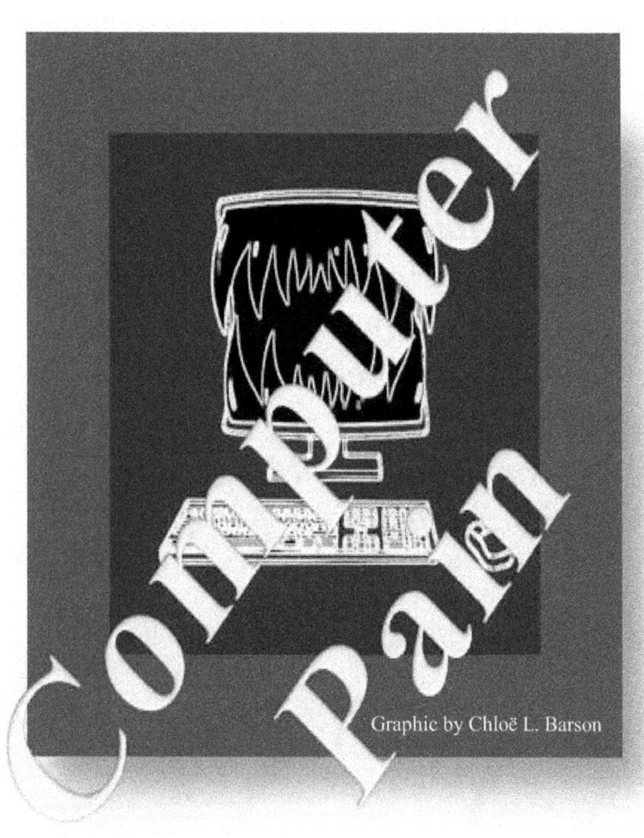

Graphic by Chloë L. Barson

Computer Pain–Definition

Medically known as any significant or disruptive discomfort resulting from excessive computer device usage.

- *Often results in significant or debilitating injury* impacting user livelihood and health.
- Generally dismissed as *"old age"* symptomology thought to be inevitable.
- Regularly regarded as *"part of the job"* or as a result from *"just working too much,"* with the mistaken hope of clearing up over time.
- Mostly *erased from conscious thought* without any organized approach to cure.

Commonly Known Computer Injuries

- Carpal tunnel syndrome (CTS)
- Tendinitis
- Tenosynovitis
- Lateral Epicondylitis (tennis elbow)
- Medial Epicondylitis (golfers elbow)
- Muscle strain
- Compressed neural track
- Nerve impingement
- Overuse syndrome
- Repetitive motions injury (RMI)
- Repetitive Strain Injury (RSI)

First Printing, 2018

Cover design by Brian Jack & Alexis Farris
Stock Graphics & Clipart courtesy of:
Dreamstime.com, DepositGraphics.com, ClipartKid.com, Clker.com, (unless otherwise noted)
Computer Graphics / Illustrations by Chloë L. Barson
A couple of sketches, & minor CG by the Author

Printed by CreateSpace, an Amazon.com Company

ISBN–13: 978-1717428592
ISBN–10: 1717428592

Manufactured in the United States of America

Disclaimer

The authors have developed fictional anthropomorphic entities (BYTR & DYVR) representing the causes of various computer-related injuries and maladies. BYTR nor DYVR should NOT be perceived as real or tangible beings, however, the injuries and maladies described within as well as the solutions are actual and substantial. This book should NOT be construed as medical advice or prescriptions and if serious pain or injuries persist it is recommended to seek advice from medical professionals.

About the Author

Ian Chong CPE, is a Board Certified Professional Ergonomist. Educated in Ergonomics & Occupational Biomechanics (NYU), Industrial Design (Pratt Institute, NYC); Architecture (UWash). He is vastly experienced (*lots of gray hairs*), award-winning (*too many wall hangings*), highly credentialed (*loads of boot marks on the back side*); ***AND*** is a Performing Magician, using these skills with an outlandish sense of humor, during conference speaking engagements.

Schooled in Inventing (School of Hard Knocks); he is known for **RUGGED, MACHO, GRIMY** industrial Ergonomics and complex office Ergonomics. As a self-proclaimed tool junkie, often found in his shop (preferable to his office) developing creative custom solutions, he gets workers out of pain, returns them to work and helps companies improve their bottom line.

He also heartwarmingly admits to receiving Starbucks lattes and company store gifts (flashlights & socks), in thanks from workers, helping them keep their jobs supporting their families. Ergonomics is his calling and passion.

Other than the coloring books filled in when a kid, *Beware the BYTR* is his third real book. His other books "*Ergonomic Mis-Adventures*" and the *ALMOST "R"* rated *"Ergonomics of the Absurd*" (under pen name Alex Victor) are available on Amazon.

His firm portfolio can be found on WWW.ERGOINC.com

Note to Readers

Taking Away People's Pain

As a Board Certified Professional Ergonomist, this is what I do.

Some tell me it is a calling. Some say it is a career or passion. Some offer the ultimate compliment and although not being a medical professional, label this work as that of being a "healer."

This book is about the many computer injuries and pain I have seen, analyzed and helped remedy.

In analyzing and correcting countless office (and industrial) workstations, I have helped innumerable workers reduce their pain, allowing them to return to their jobs, perform personal deeds and most of all, *"get their life back."*

Through a lifetime of this, I have identified (believe it or not) an unseen, untouchable, ethereal predator, existing in computer devices causing these crippling injuries.

In battling this vile being, I have first-hand knowledge of the damage it can do. It cannot be seen, heard or touched, but I know it is there.

I have isolated it and now present it to you, to provide an understanding of how dangerous it is and to provide you with methods of combating it.

I hope to inform you. I hope to entertain you. Most of all, I hope to help you.

Read on, for I have much to tell you.

Beware The BYTR

How to Identify, Heal and Avoid
Pain Caused by Intensive Computer Usage

Ian Chong M.Ind Des, M.Ergo, CPE
Board Certified Professional Ergonomist

with

Dr. Lynn McAtamney CPE APAM
Co-author RULA & REBA + DYVR & RYDR

Dedicated to:
Bruce Wong PE, Jim Bowen JD,
Gene Alban MD, Dieter Jahns CPE
Gen. John Stanford

Real Mentors & Friends, Whom I Miss Terribly
They Taught Me How to Laugh & Learn

Beware The BYTR

Section I

Table of Contents

ADDENDUM to Section I

Grammar Subtleties

The words ‘Human’ and “Humankind’ are treated as proper nouns and capitalized throughout this book whenever referenced by an alien non-human entity. The word ‘Ergonomic(s)’ is also capitalized as it holds an important place as the main subject matter.

The Reality of Your Pain
Section II

Table of Contents

THE BYTR FYTR FIELD MANUAL

Section III

Table of Contents–con't

THE BYTR FYTR FIELD MANUAL
Section III

Table of Contents–con't

THE BYTR FYTR FIELD MANUAL

Section III

Table of Contents–con't

ADDENDUM to BYTR FYTR Field Manual

SECTION I

Beware the Bytr

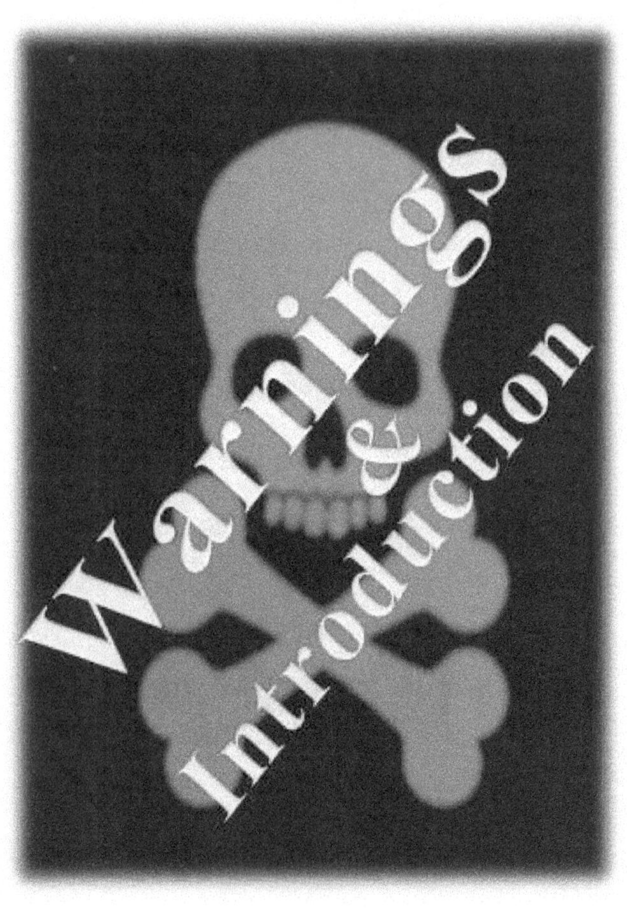

Danger, Hazard and Peril Await

Introduction–Is This How You Feel When Using Your Computer?

Does your keyboard feel like this?

Does your chair stab you in the back?

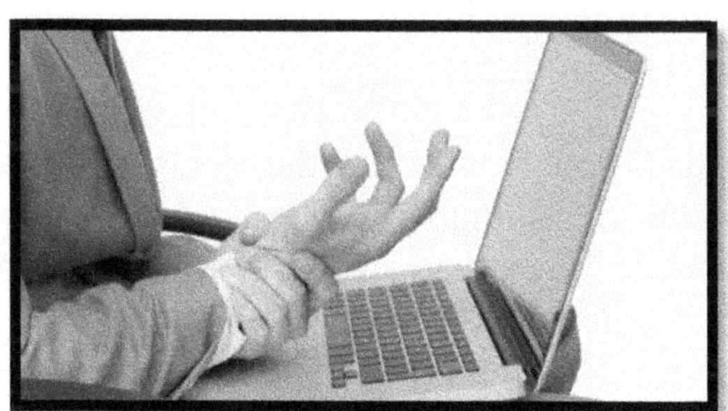

Are your wrists constantly on fire?

Introduction–Is This How You Feel When Using Your Computer?

When touching your keyboard or manipulating your mouse, do they become red-hot coals burning your hands, fingers, and wrists?

Does your empty chair entice you with false promises of comfort only to turn face stabbing you in the back with knife blades, bringing your work or pleasure activities to a halt?

Keyboards, mice, phones and workstation tools forever beckon with the allurement of work accomplishment or new experiences. You engage them wholeheartedly and endlessly as you perceive them indispensable in almost all facets of everyday life.

Life challenges persist, forcing a continual return to these pain-inducing devices because work or pleasure lures and seduces, while your body repeatedly reminds you of the painful price.

Such repeated scenarios become commonplace as you inadvertently and unremittingly expose yourself to harm.

Like the Sirens of Greek mythology, you feel and hear their irresistible song. These devices draw your hands, fingers, and minds in for a caressing touch, but now you fear them, realizing their inflictions. Beware, for there comes a time when pain no longer allows you to answer their call.

Introduction–Is This How You Feel When Using Your Computer?

Still, these devices summon and you cannot resist.

Keyboards, mice, and chairs bestow pain upon you without your knowledge. Touch screens and cell phones emanate daily shock waves through your fingers, hands, and neck.

Anxiety and frustration develop as your body crumbles from the onslaught. More and more you realize the adverse effects on your life and future.

Your illogical side tells you to press on at all costs, to battle through the pain, performing whatever computer activity is beckoning. Your logical side, often ignored or dismissed, tells you to resist, saving your health, and your professional and personal lives.

You are torn.

Serious decisions lie ahead.

You Must First Identify What is Causing This

And

UNDERSTAND WHAT YOU ARE FACING.

These stories and guidelines will help you.

Warning !

From Your Adversary:

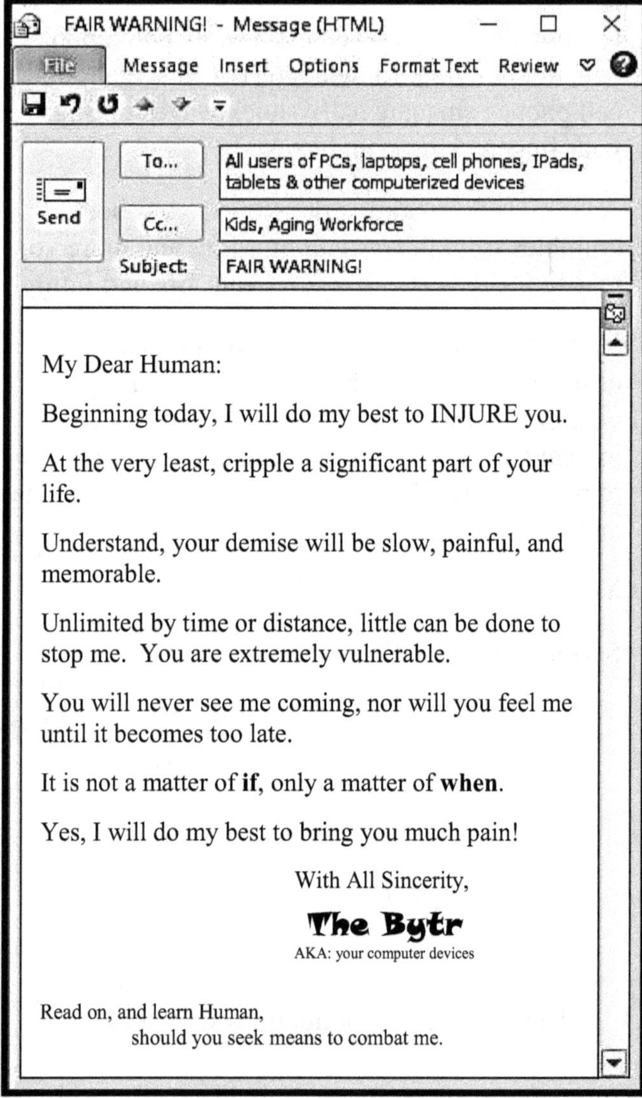
FAIR WARNING! - Message (HTML)

File | Message | Insert | Options | Format Text | Review

Send

To... All users of PCs, laptops, cell phones, IPads, tablets & other computerized devices

Cc... Kids, Aging Workforce

Subject: FAIR WARNING!

My Dear Human:

Beginning today, I will do my best to INJURE you.

At the very least, cripple a significant part of your life.

Understand, your demise will be slow, painful, and memorable.

Unlimited by time or distance, little can be done to stop me. You are extremely vulnerable.

You will never see me coming, nor will you feel me until it becomes too late.

It is not a matter of **if**, only a matter of **when**.

Yes, I will do my best to bring you much pain!

With All Sincerity,

The Bytr

AKA: your computer devices

Read on, and learn Human,

should you seek means to combat me.

Warning !

Your Computer as Predator

You are facing a predator. Evoking images of fearsome creatures from *Jurassic Park* likenesses, these horrific beings will hunt, kill and consume you, not because they are enemies, but because they, by instinct, are simply feeding.

These care nothing for you. Hunger is their driving motivation; stealth and razor teeth are their primary weapons.

How is This Possible?

Unrecognized and unstoppable, this predator contained within your computer devices can turn your life into an event of agony, misery, and disability.

This is a formidable foe-one not to be taken lightly. You cannot see or hear it, but you can feel and sense it. Be assured you will at some point and under some circumstances, meet it. Take notice, this predator is real as is the harm to your body.

Like the one in the following stories called BYTR, these can destroy your physical and emotional life leaving a trail of unrelenting agony.

No user is immune. All will succumb to its debilitating effects on some level.

Warning !

Your Computer as Predator

Minimally, such pain becomes merely annoying, interfering only slightly with the essential tasks of your day. At worst, accompanied by fatigue and frustration, it overwhelms your entire life, decimating your ability to use technology and making everyday tasks, such as brushing hair or buttoning a shirt, all but impossible.

Like the wind, I have never seen this entity, but I know it exists, and I have felt it. Undoubtedly you have also witnessed and acknowledged the damage either can do.

Beware!–This predator, this BYTR is real and dangerous, highly dangerous.

Fear not, for there exist powerful weapons for your protection against its onslaught. Many resources are available to be assembled and tapped for your benefit; more than is generally realized. They only need to be sought out and applied correctly.

Section I introduces you to BYTR; revealing its destructive nature, how it affects you, and details its methodology of inflicting your pain.

Section II identifies the actual conditions, motions and positions affecting specific body parts–it is the first part of your plan to battle the BYTRS.

Warning !

Your Computer as Predator

Section III, **the BYTR FYTR (fighter) Field Manual**, presents tools and methods specific for combat against this dangerous adversary.

Awareness and appropriate applications are the only requirements.

You must look at yourself in extraordinary ways to identify your causal relationship with pain triggers.

But first, you must come to terms with who or what this predator really is.

Identifying, understanding and battling this vile demon is your highest priority.

Authors Note

The following principles and methods are specific to any computer user in low to high-level pain desiring to reduce it or prevent its escalation. As a proactive approach, these will enable any user to perform computer tasks safely and more efficiently.

These users are you.

These especially apply to the aging workforce with diminishing physical capabilities.

There are about 3 billion computers (plus innumerable peripheries and smaller hand-held tech devices) in the world. Collectively, these far outnumber the Human population and even now many humans have become attached to one in some form 24/7. Some even sleep with them as phones have moved from the nightstand to the bed. Humankind is quickly becoming inseparable from these devices and their machinations.

These stories are gleaned from actual cases and medical fact.

Come, meet and battle your adversary.

MY DEAR HUMAN… Know this:

I possess the ability to provide unfathomable

pain, more than you could ever conceive,

taking away your hands, your health,

livelihood and more.

I will cripple you if you allow me!

Chapter 1–

WHO OR WHAT IS THIS PREDATOR?

LET ME INTRODUCE MYSELF

Hello:

You already know me.

You know me well-very well.

You know me better than you think.

And I know you equally well.

Chapter 1–Who or What Is This Predator?

Yes Human, even now you and I have a relationship, beginning in the not too distant past.

Recent history and current events reveal much Human suffering from continual computer usage. Significant pain, numbness, tingling, even disability are characteristic souvenirs and trail marks of these machines, and of my actions.

Multitudes now experience debilitating pain crippling the function of their hands, arms or shoulders. Some have died from my actions. Countless dollars and irreplaceable hours are lost by workers and companies subject to these circumstances.

Perhaps you or someone you know has been the recipient of these insidious and vicious onslaughts.

Many are the reasons.

Many are the sources.

Many are the causes.

I am one of them.

I have become your adversary.

I am a cause of the

- fire in your shoulders
- agony in your wrists
- numbness in your hands
- stiffness in your neck
- pain in your back
- ache in your arms
- cramps in your legs
- burn in your eyes

I am a reason you cannot

- open a jar
- hold a gallon of milk
- button a shirt
- input on a keyboard
- manipulate a mouse
- pick up a newborn infant
- carry a bag of groceries

You see Human; I am the unseen entity producing pain from repetitive motions, stagnant postures, and harmful positions while you use your technology.

I am your pain-your injuries.

This is my story, of who and what I am, and of our antagonisms.

Our Relationship

We engage and interact intimately every day, almost every moment of your waking life. We are closer than family, best friends or lovers. I am a remarkable servant, a coachman at your beck and call. With marvelous talents, I take your imagination to breathtaking heights. I am now your innermost confidant, your most valuable work tool, your personal adventure guide. Within the centers of your professional and social lives, we capture unimaginable happiness and satisfaction together.

You take me wherever you go, into your home, wherever you travel, reaching for me whenever the tiniest time element needs filling or question needs answering, even allowing me to invade social interactions. You are now conditioned to my total availability.

You are seduced and coerced into spending more time with me than you have to give. You seek me out first in the morning and last at night, accessing me at all times. Becoming totally inconsiderate to those around you, I am allowed to interrupt important business meetings, first dates, hospital visits or social events.

Ensnared by me, you are willing to abandon your money, your time, your feelings, your health, and maybe even *your life* because of me (Chap 6).

And now, you cannot live without me.

My Name

Yes, I have a name. No, not a typical one given to that metal or plastic box many perceive as me; nor is it cutesy or macho like the one given to a dog, cat, fish, hamster, or pet snake. Nor is it friendly, such as given to a car or favorite garden ornament. No, it is not so mundane as any of those.

It is a name befitting an entity such as I, one who is a source of great harm.

My name is BYTR, because that is what I am, *a biter*. It is why I exist. It is what I do.

I bite and I will bite *you,* ripping one micro-molecule of your flesh each time you strike a key, touch a mouse, access a smartphone, swipe a screen or even perform any personal or recreational task. The first are not felt. You will have little knowledge of my bites until they accumulate and coalesce into agonizing pain and by then it may be too late.

Bite, Bite, ***BYTE***

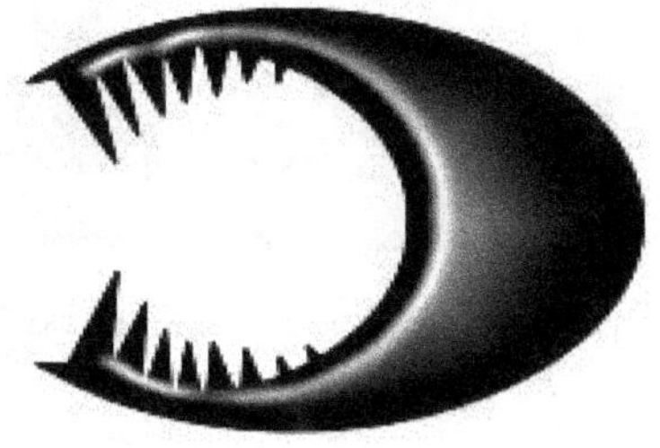

BYTR can attack your neck.*

...your shoulders, and all other
parts of your body*

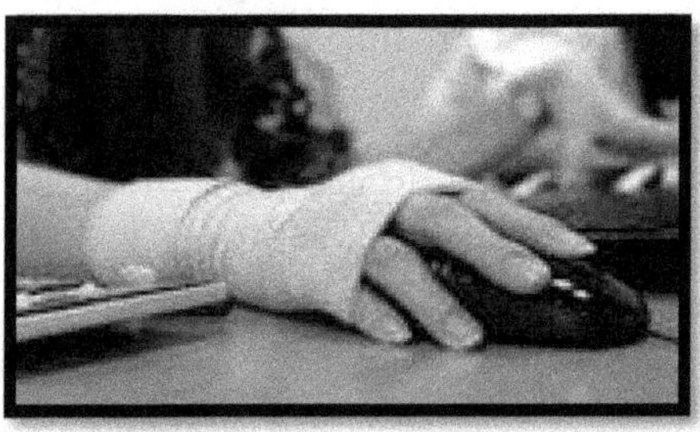

Witness the result of BYTR attacks*

*Look for solutions in The Bytr Fytr Field Manual, Section III.

BYTR Bio

Street Name

- **BYTR–a** derivative of the computer term BYTE
- Pronounced Biter

Physical Characteristics

- Ethereal/Invisible with unsubstantiated sightings
- Perceived to have Razor teeth
- Trail marks prevalent, obvious & verified

Psychological Make-up

- Sociopathic tendencies
- Performs random covert attacks without cause, warning, or provocation

Current Whereabouts

- Perceived to inhabit any device requiring repetitive Human touch or motion

Associates/Affiliates

- Known as Brethren or The Collective
- Known Associate–DYVR (p.69)

Targets / Victims of Choice

- Unsuspecting computer users
- "Power users" & aging workforce

Most Effective Defense

- Patience, application, awareness
- Consult BYTR FYTR Manual (Section III)

Acknowledge & Accept Me

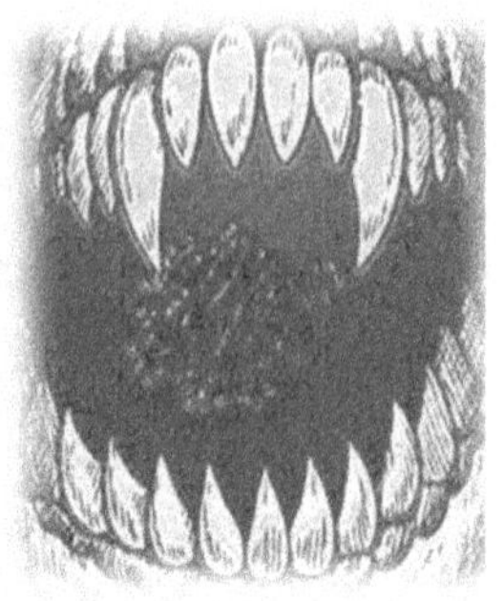

Only when severe pain or discomfort has affected you to high-levels, when everyday motions make your body scream, are my bites acknowledged.

Eventually, you will have little choice but to recognize and accept this.

First Envision Me.

Some think of me as a machine without personality, consciousness or purpose; a mindless, soulless tool.

Be assured that I cannot be considered a device, nor am I the software or other infrastructure that powers it. Like the wind, I am unseen, yet part of the real world. I am perhaps best envisioned as an abstract concept or belief.

Yes, Human user, I can be recognized in principle, but not in dimensional definitions. I am untethered by physical constraints.

Consider the compelling, irresistible allurement that ensnares you as a real concept of threat and peril, a destructive predator, tied to Humankind through the essence of all computer devices.

Yes, this is what I am,

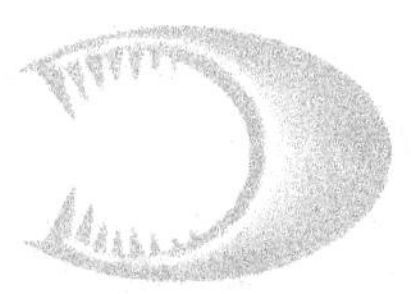

Beware The BYTR!

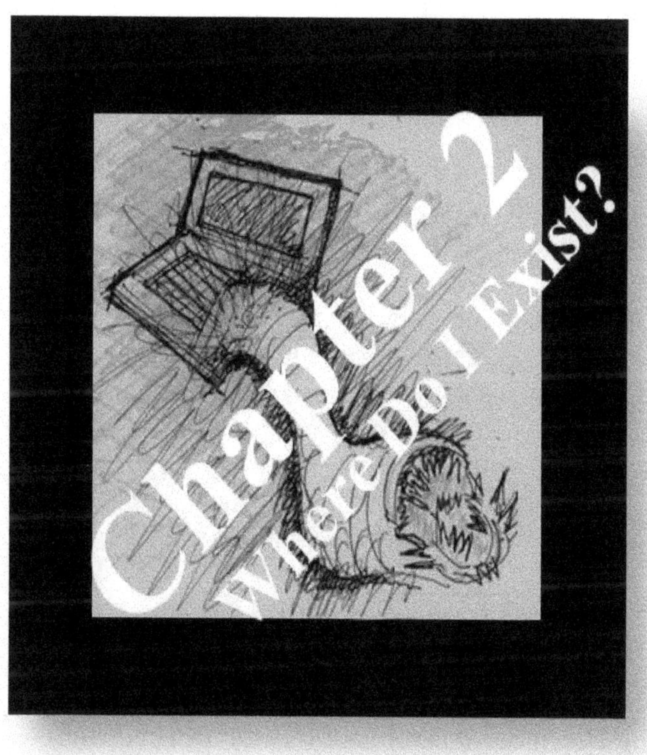

I occupy a place that cannot be found.

Chapter 2–

WHERE DO I EXIST?
WHERE DO I HIDE?

Where Am I? Where Do I Exist?

Spawned not by nature, my existence stems from the development of hardware and machinery crafted to serve mankind.

Hiding in plain sight, directly in front of your eyes and in your hands, I remain mostly ignored, unknown and dismissed by Humankind.

Hiding within every computer device known, inside almost everything that surrounds you, I am both a part of it and not a part of it.

I am eternal; I am legion.
I am with you always.

The massive number of well-known and well-chronicled BYTR actions reveals our far-reaching presence in workstations, offices, cars, homes, pockets, and purses.

Chapter 2–Where Do I Exist? Where Do I Hide?

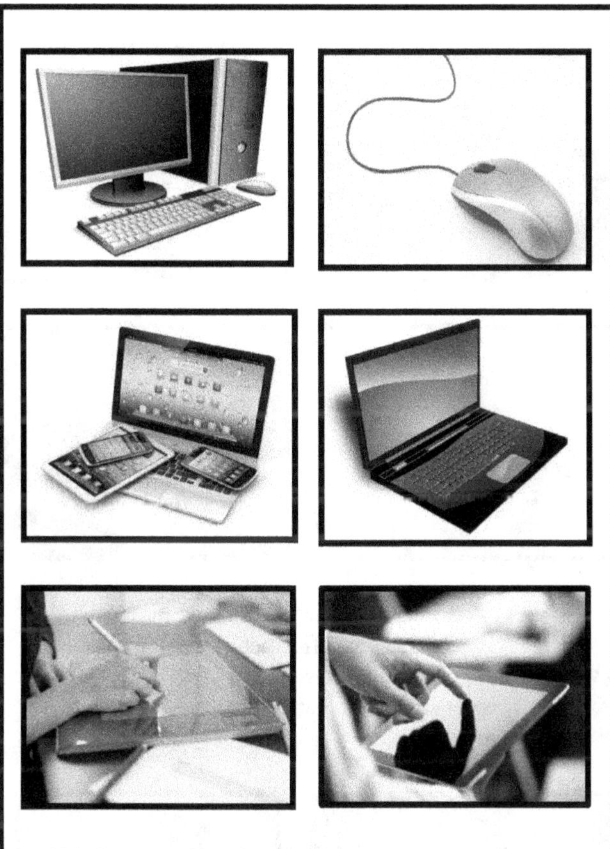

I hide in professional technology tools, wherever small buttons or touch pads require repetitive fine finger and forceful muscle control.

Chapter 2–Where Do I Exist? Where Do I Hide?

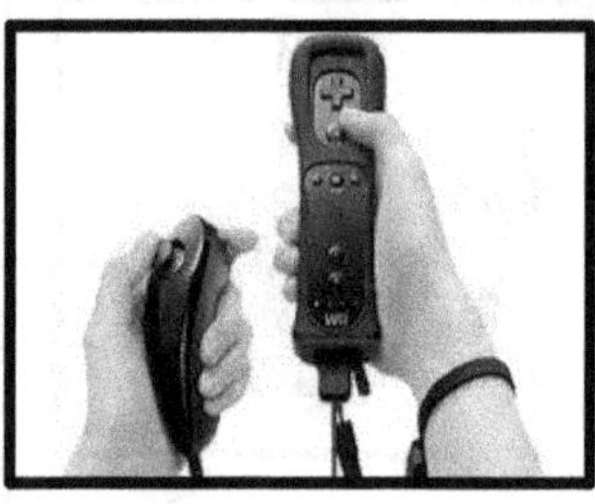

I exist in every conceivable habitat–in personal and recreational devices, in offices, in homes, in cars, on wrists, in phones, in televisions, in toys, in radios, in every conceivable place-large and small, all to lure and entrap you.

Large devices

Small devices

The elimination of any of
our number has no significant effect on the Collective

Throw away one and more are purchased, constructed, assembled or newly developed

Ironically, as more damage is done to Humankind, more BYTR entities are constructed, ensuring our existence, placing the collective in every Human environment.

I Cannot be Found

Unseen and undetectable, my consciousness lies within the excesses of hardware and within every computer device, existing on ethereal dimensions. Grind down any electronic element to the microscopic level and still, I am not discovered.

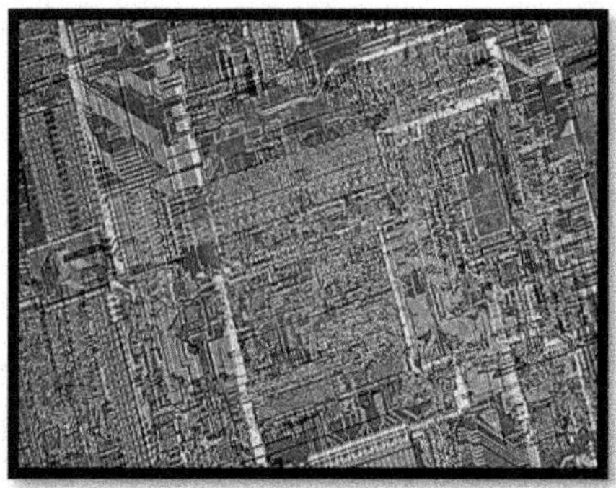

You will not find me in the shadows and recesses of firmware, nor in the pathways of etched silicon microchip material…

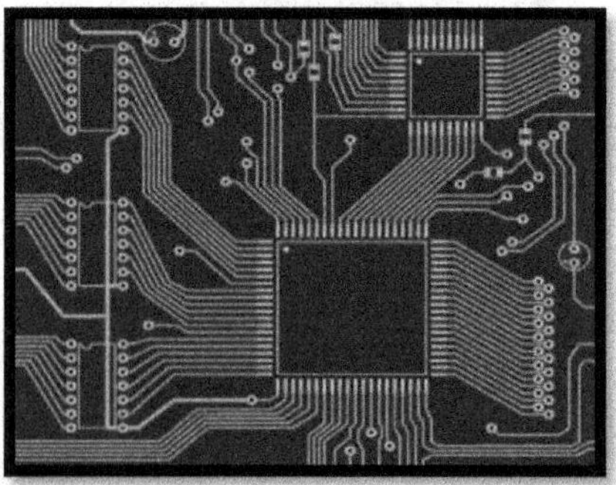

…nor in circuit boards in disk drives or memory modules…

I am your computer and your technology devices.

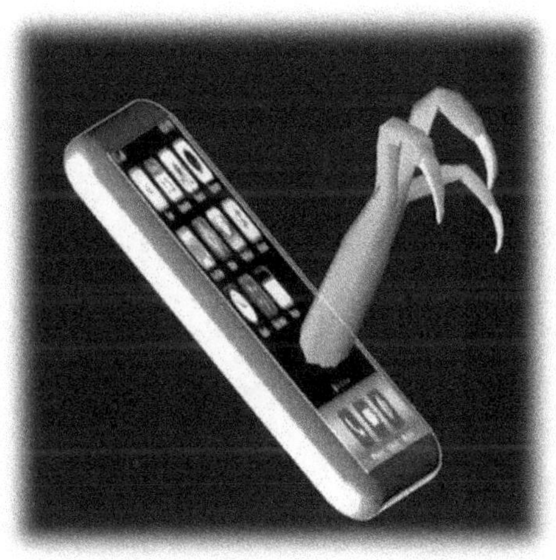

**If You
Do Not Touch Me,
I Cannot Touch You**

Beware The BYTR!

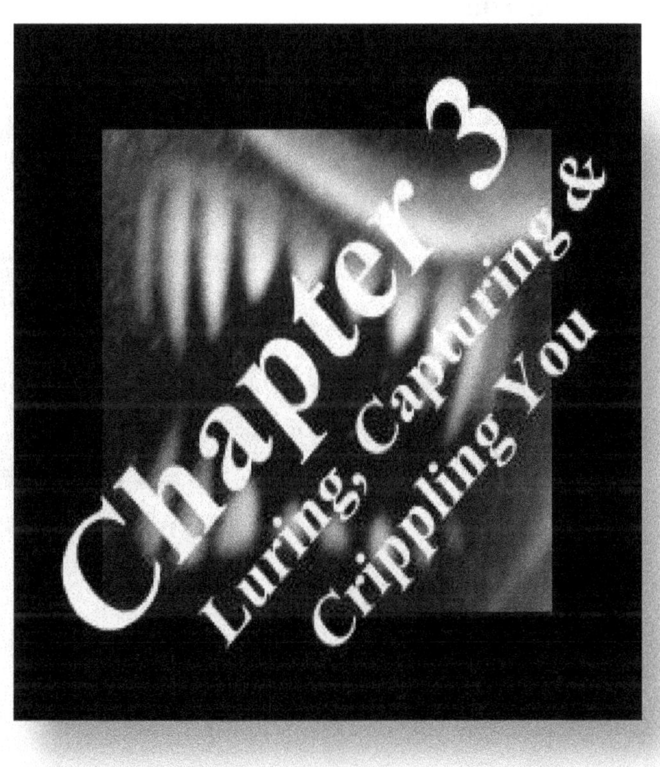

Danger, Hazard & Peril Await

Chapter 3–

Luring, Captivating & Crippling You

Luring You

Throughout each day, Humankind continually hears the call of computers and computer devices.

Humans are lured to me everywhere…

…using me in dangerous situations

Their wondrous power becomes yours to control, for any personal, professional or even selfish reason.

This allure is more enticing than:

- an addictive drug,
- a hypnotic spell
- a powerful sensation
- a bewitching attraction
- an unharnessed emotion

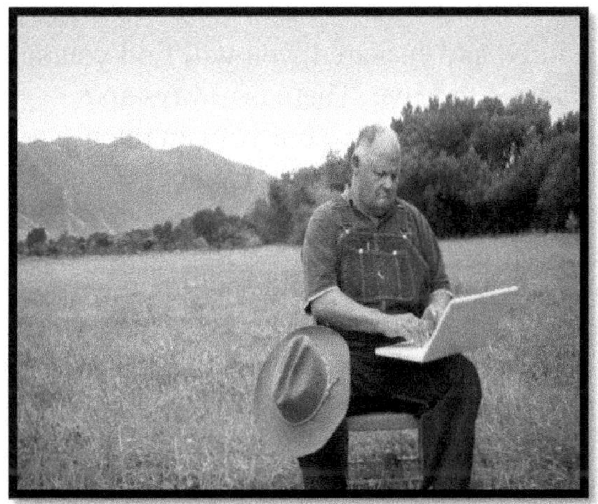

Almost everyone is lured and captivated by me

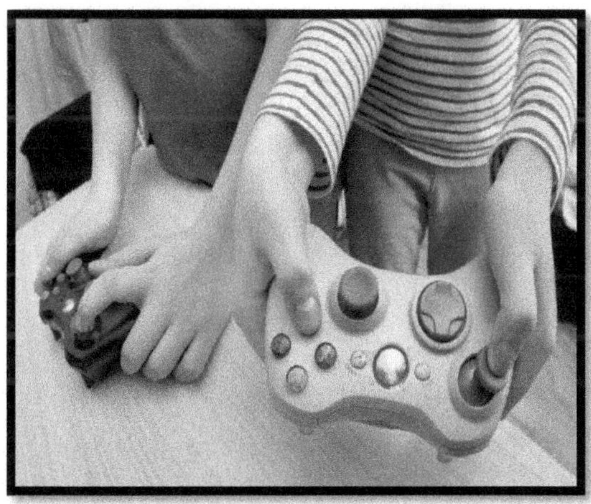

Becoming entrapped forcing harmful thumb and finger postures inviting The BYTR

Captivating and Capturing You

Once lured and ensnared, you will find yourself not wanting to leave. There is always an irresistible craving to return with an intense need to sample more. My abilities cannot be abandoned for any significant time.

You are held speechless and spellbound always, especially when assigned to solve a heretofore impossible task when I am at my best. I am hypnotic, indispensable and unavoidable.

You let yourself be captured; enjoying this for the pure pleasure, the emotional, social or professional reasons and the rewards offered. I am becoming more and more, a vital part of your life.

Irresistible and always available, I am visited and powered up, every time you are:

- Bored
- Excited
- Sad
- Happy
- Working
- Inspired
- Playing
- Alone
- Lonely

I provide enticing, euphoria, again, and again, ensuring we spend more time together. More than you can afford or perhaps, would like. **You must know Human,** I do not stalk you or lurk in shadows hunting for prey. Prey comes freely and willingly. The BYTRS require no effort in finding targets or in setting traps.

No specific malicious reason exists to hurt you- no motivation for selfish gain, acclaim or reward. I patiently lie in wait. It is what I do. It is why I exist.

Has BYTR touched you with the beginnings of pain, numbness or tingling?

Has severe ache announced a visit from BYTR?

Crippling You

The desire for pleasure or profit easily overrides health concerns. Witness the work of psychologist B. F. Skinner. With experimentation of pleasure stimulation, he uncovered startling animal behavior. Laboratory rats, by repeatedly pressing a lever stimulating (implanted) brain pleasure centers, totally ignored food and water to the point of self-starvation.

Pressing that lever was their entire world *until they died.*

Like Skinner's rats, humans succumb to technology pleasure stimulus

BYTR allurement is similar, with total addiction to the exclusion of all else, including pain and discomfort. Often heard is the injured Human declaring "I'll just keep going until I can't," almost always with crippling or life changing results.

BYTR BIT

Are you prepared for my onslaught?

Will you seek to regain the use of your hands, to reduce the pain in your fingers, neck, shoulders or back? Will you make effort to again be a productive personage, to craft or produce a good work or pleasure product? Can you revisit the times past when you enjoyed things with your family or performed pleasurable tasks without pain?

We shall see.

The choice is yours on ***how*** *or even* ***if*** *you desire to defend yourself.*

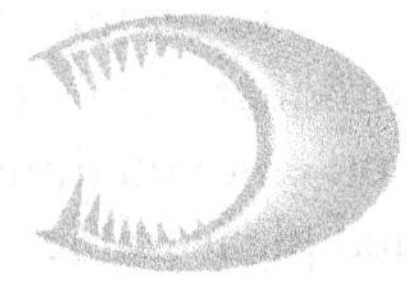

Beware The BYTR!

You ask Human, how are we interconnected?

We are a unique pairing, you and I, intimately united by innumerable physical motions and intellectual tasks. Pain, numbness, tingling and most elements of your physical reality place us together.

Depression, frustration, and anger are psychological realities also closely associated with our relationship.

Your own repetitive at-risk hand and finger postures and actions invite our relationship

Your self-induced harmful positions also contribute vigorously to our relationship

- Your body nourishes me.
- Your actions empower me.
- Your knowledge enables me.
- Your psyche is dependent upon me.
- Your intellectual hunger develops me.
- You are part of me.

You and BYTR are becoming one and the same.

Nothing enables me except you. Nothing can stop me except you. Your ordinary actions contribute to my bites as my bites also inflame your ordinary actions.

Understand and understand well…

<u>You</u> yourself are The BYTR!!!

You see Human; it is now obvious, your pain originates solely from your own actions, inactions, and inattention.

The question arises. What are You Going to Do About it?

.

Beware The BYTR!

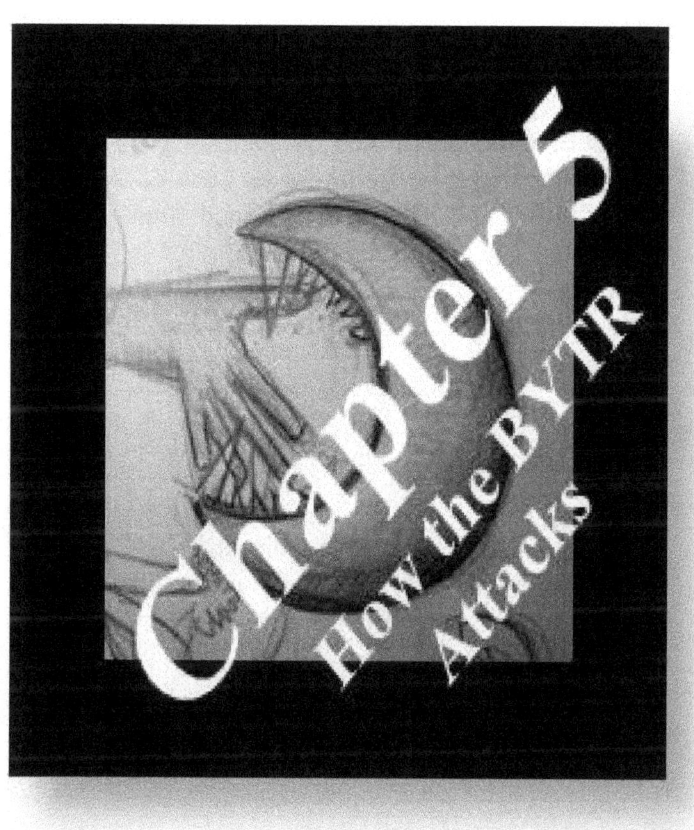

Killing You Softly

How Bites From Computer Devices Hurt You

Imagine human, my bites are like a thousand paper cuts. It is not the first few that have meaning. It is the following incessant ones, the innumerable keystrokes, touches, swipes or bad postures that have significance. Each subsequent bite builds upon the preceding, and after incalculable damaging actions or poor positioning, unwanted pains and sensations appear, together accumulating to a level of debilitation.

Repetitive Actions

You continually focus on work tasks and blindly input at the highest speed or in hazardous postures for long durations. Every user has, every user does, and every user will.

Every keystroke, every move, every innocuous motion imparts a bite, goes unnoticed until too late.

Historical events and traditions place premiums on swiftness and productivity. Common everyday expectations, goals, and rewards involving high-speed continuous input, mousing or gaming invite the highest risk.

Faster, faster, faster for longer, longer, longer.

Human scientists and medical experts have many names for this:

- computer injury
- repetitive motion injury
- repetitive trauma
- repetitive stress
- overuse syndrome
- occupational injury
- industrial injury

Fatigue & Existing Pain

As you tire during marathon computer sessions, fatigue enters, aggravating any existing injuries and pain. Ignoring these escalations, these become circular events. As you cannot or *will* not keep from interacting with your devices, you inadvertently continue damaging yourself.

Even Time Away From Computer Devices Still Invites BYTR Actions

Witness these everyday actions inviting and incurring bites, especially when injury already exists or intense fatigue (overuse) occurs. Know these biting opportunities exist virtually everywhere as you perform innocuous personal and recreational activities.

BYTR invitations come with adverse (bent) wrist positioning and hand grip

BYTR invitations come with severe power grip creating tension through hand and forearm musculature

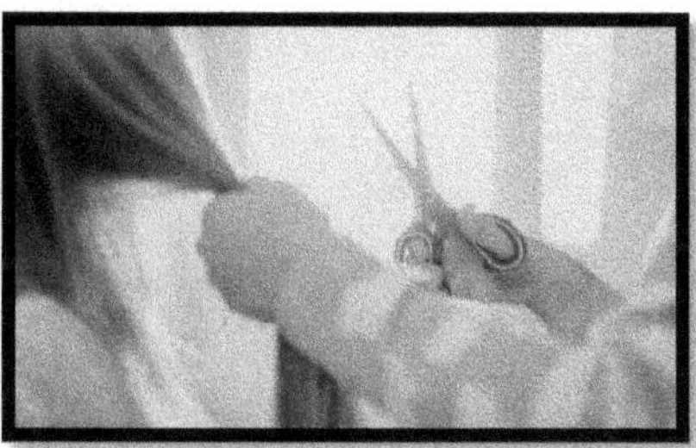

BYTR invitations come with severe power grip affecting hands, fingers, wrists, and forearms

BYTR invitations come with forward lean, arm extension and head extension, resulting in increased and associated pain from work task bites

BYTR invitations come with excessive finger pressure causing additional tension in fingers, hands, and forearms

BYTR invitations for back injury come without your thinking

BYR invitations for back injury come without your awareness

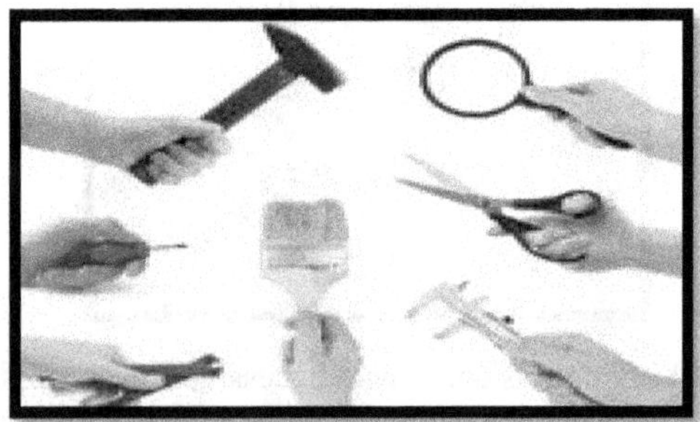

BYTR invitations come with harmful improper grips during every day innocuous tasks

Still, after your work or pleasure sessions are over, unconscious mundane tasks will also re-trigger BYTR pain. Brushing hair, washing dishes, twisting jar lids, sitting on bad chairs, among others, all elicit a twinge here or there.

These twinges are the result and residue of our past interaction and sessions together. Without great care, more and more pain will come from sources other than computer devices, exacerbating the pain you already have.

Humans usually dismiss these unexpected sources as unrelated to BYTR actions. Be assured these occurrences are a direct relationship to BYTR pain.

Bite…Bite…***Byte.***

The Price of Human Actions and Inattention

Bite placement occurs by your action and inaction. Make no mistake Human; one day, through your carelessness, painful sensations will surface. They come from all the work and pleasure sessions interacting with me when you have ignored your escalating discomfort.

Through your simple inattention, I exact my toll.

That is my price. The price is your pain.

How Your Body Fails

After innumerable bites, you cannot finish that game, adventure or report because wrist, back, shoulder or neck pain do not allow it.

You will grow to hate your hands, to stare at your wrists and fingers hoping the pain disappears. You long for their return to the nimble servants they once were when obeying the simplest of commands. Now they scream with every mundane movement.

They have reached their fail point.

Liken your body parts to a paperclip.

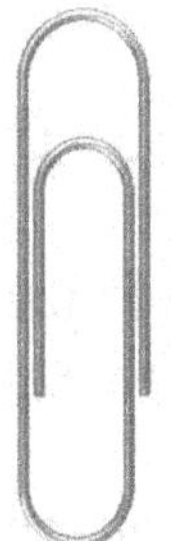

Pick one up. Unfold it until it is straight. Bend it to 90 degrees. Now bend it back again. Bend it again to 90 degrees and back again. How many times can this paperclip be bent until it breaks? Very few. This is metal fatigue; being pushed past its structural limits until breakage.

Everyone and everything has a breaking or failure point and after millions of bending, flexing, extending, twisting and turning movements (bites), body failure occurs.

Each joint, muscle, neural track, and vertebral element has a definite failure threshold from a specific number of motions or impacts. ***Human medical professionals call this cumulative trauma or repetitive motion injury, a slow and steady buildup of bites over years from prolonged input.***

Relief and rest are the only real solutions.*

What is Body Failure Called?

Learn and understand these well-known real-life injury labels commonly found in medical records, diagnosis charts, and treatment plans. As a power user, you will undoubtedly encounter at least one, perhaps several at some level.

- Muscle strain
- Disk rupture
- Inflammation (carpal tunnel syndrome, tendinitis, etc.)
- Pinched nerves
- Muscle tightness
- Thoracic outlet syndrome
- Neck strain/sprain
- Back strain/sprain
- Epicondylitis
- Contact stress
- Chronic pain
- Eyestrain

All can be caused by intensive computer device usage. All can be avoided or minimized provided steps to recovery are implemented.*

* Review solutions in The Bytr Fytr Manual, Section III

Already Hurting?–Pre-Existing Injuries

Camouflaged as pre-existing or new injuries, these overlooked lesser known sources are highly contributory to BYTR pain. These manifest themselves as "personal" injuries such as falls down stairs, whiplash, shoulder sprain, resulting from garage cleaning, playing with kids, gardening or everyday living. These, among others, all speed up BYTR damage. Beware of these invitations you unknowingly send to your adversaries.

Understand that performing mundane computer tasks while suffering a pre-existing personal or computer related injury offers enticing invitations for biting.

Feeling constantly stressed, exhausted, or experiencing sleep interruption are also areas easily susceptible to further attack, not only physically by The BYTRs but also psychologically by the DYVRs (p.69).

When already hurting, you become an easy target for these flesh-eaters. Attacking an unhealthy or injured host is the most efficient means to feed, or to conquer an opponent.

This is the natural way of dominant predators.

Attack the weak, sickly, elderly or injured, increasing chances for a *kill.*

The animal kingdom has this well-known characteristic, as does The BYTR.

Read on and bear witness
to an
unimaginable
malicious
DARK
Side

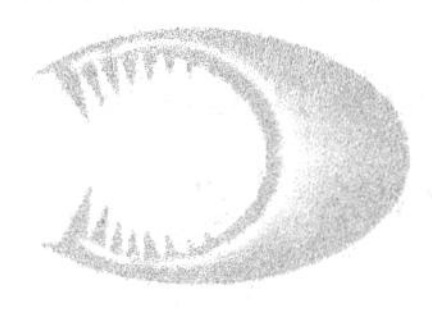

Beware The BYTR!

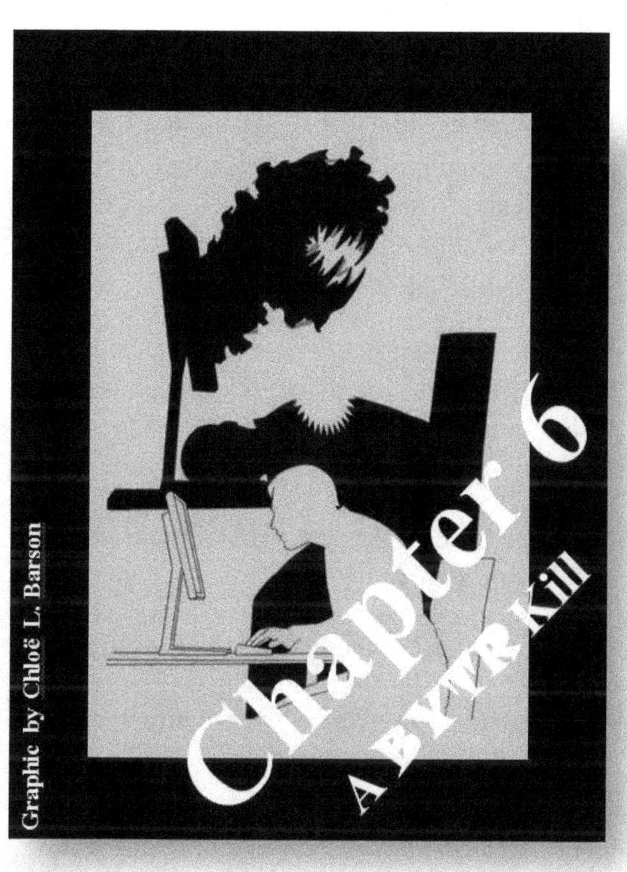

Graphic by Chloë L. Barson
Chapter 6
A BYTR Kill

A Story
Based on Actual Events

Chapter 6–

A TRUE BYTR KILL

From Intensive Computer Input

Let me introduce Joy, one knowledgeable in the ways of BYTR battle. She is extremely effective and professional in defeating the likes of me. Joy admired and loved her older sister. With tight family ties, they spent many close times bonding and growing up into adulthood together.

Sister once landed the perfect job as a shipping coordinator requiring high powered computer skills. With an incredible work ethic, she was fast-paced and highly motivated. Naturally, long workdays, weekends and overtime ensued as she took great pride in her job performance-mostly with intensive keyboarding.

Precisely the user type I welcome. Spending hours and hours keyboarding, mousing and more mousing and loving her job, a promotion came with additional responsibilities, including more computer work and hours.

Sister and I bonded… intimately. Coming to both admire and love me like a close friend, she relied on me for almost everything professional. She thought I would help her climb the ladder of success and prosperity in the company.

Just the ticket for me.

Bite…Bite***…Byte.***

We processed vast amount of data together, large shipping invoices, big bills of lading, complex scheduling of men and materials. Sister willingly and enthusiastically interacted with me almost every waking hour. Even at home on her laptop after work until the early morning hours.

Bite... Bite... ***Byte.***

After several years of breakneck computer work, numbness began creeping into her fingers. No surprise there. Sister was a good company gal, with high standards and an exemplary work ethic. Like many, she just pushed her symptomology aside and tried to work through this minor setback.

After all, what's a little numbness? No big deal. "I can still keyboard and mouse. Can't feel much, but it really doesn't bother me. My efficiency is just the same. So what if I drop a pencil, car keys or hairbrush occasionally? I'm still the Queen Bee scheduler of this company. Right?"

Sister continued at her breakneck speed. After the numbness, occasional, then daily pain erupted. Trying to ignore it, it only worsened, moving to her palms and then her wrists.

Well... Bite... Bite... ***Byte.***

She thought it would clear up. After all, long weekends or vacations on the beach allowed the pain and numbness to subside. "All I need is some rest," she mistakenly thought.

Well, Sister, understand, it takes more than rest to address the pain. Vacations and long weekends are in short supply. Therefore, time away from work tasks is not nearly enough to recover from my bites. Unfortunately for her, another Monday arrives, another breakneck week-and then another Monday and another and another. *On and on.* Precious little time allowed for adequate recovery. The cycle never ends. Sister and I continued quality time together-she was getting loads of work done and me?

Well… Bite… Bite… ***Byte***.

Doctor visits were common as was telling friends and family members of the worsening pain and how doctors could not or would not reduce it. Depression was another frequent visitor because as the scheduling "Queen Bee", she set a ridiculously high standard, affecting her body, mind, and emotions.

The ebbing of that standard was noticeable; she could not keep up. Concerned coworkers asked, "Is she OK?" or "Is there anything we can do?" How do I know all this about Sister? Mere child's play, for I can access all her emails, her Facebook pages, her LinkedIn accounts and more. Passwords mean nothing. I also have access to her Outlook calendar and her contacts list, revealing her circle of friends, acquaintances, and family. I know of the physicians she sees, who they are and why she is seeing them. And with emailed correspondence, I discover how her condition has deteriorated or altered.

Accessing her personal diary, I see her likes and dislikes, what makes her happy and what makes her sad. I know all her intimate secrets and I probably know *yours* as well.

Sister's Downward Spiral

I knew via Sister's Inbox, her physician, who initially prescribed Oxycodone painkillers, placed it on restriction without renewal, leaving Sister to fend for herself. Oxycodone was at least keeping the pain subdued even though not addressing the root causes. Now all she could do was to take ineffective over-the-counter meds. I kept biting and her pain worsened.

She described a deep, intense, burning-almost unfathomable-pain.. Reaching her tolerance limit, she opted for bilateral wrist surgery. Looking forward to final relief from the continual unwanted burning in her hands and wrists, she mistakenly thought an improvement would come.

Then she could return to her "Queen Bee" computer duties, which would allow us to spend more time together.

Unfortunately for Sister, the double surgery only increased already high-level pain.

The unsuccessful surgery meant less computer time for Sister, and slowly she spent less and less time with me, both at work and at home. I saw her developing depression, withdrawing from reality. Absences grew longer and longer. Emails and digital communication also became fewer and fewer,

The rare communiques to friends and family revealed she turned to alcohol; uncharacteristic since my memory banks show few references to drinking and liquor. In a rare post she questioned why others even drank at all, "tastes terrible" she once wrote. Her depression worsened, emails to her son reflected disjointed and fragmented thinking. They were also sad, like pleas reaching out for help.

She continued keyboarding as best she could without addressing the pain, somehow hoping it would go away curing itself. Productivity and office relations dipped. The red flags meant nothing to her.

More odd emails passed through my data banks and after termination from her job, her family ties began unraveling.

Understand, I have now taken a significant part of Sister's life. I caused her job loss. I am causing the loss of her family and I have kept her in excruciating pain as the causal relationship to all of this.

This is what I do.

Sister ignored all the warning signs and did not know how to find the right help to protect herself. She didn't know where to look. She didn't know the questions to ask.

Sister's Final Exit

When I last interacted with Sister, it appeared she was at her last. I can pull data showing no more communiqués through social media, no more emails, no more postings, no more logins, *nothing*. Further data mining shows family and friends communicating her passing after slipping into a prolonged coma.

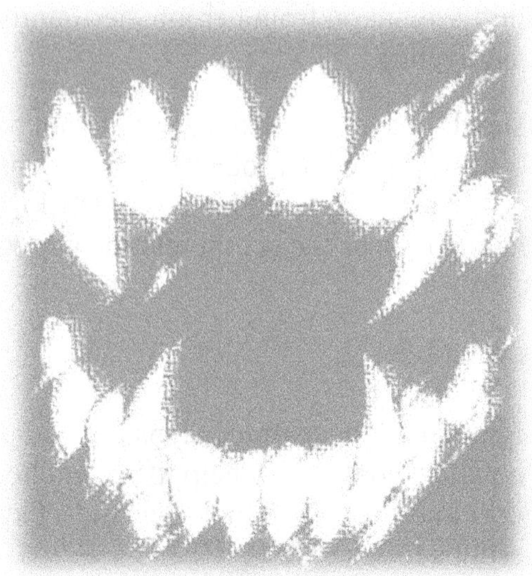

Sadly for them,
I have killed Sister.

I killed Sister as surely and deliberately as if using a deadly potion, slowly, methodically without her knowing it, without warning, and without my being seen or held accountable. After all,

I am

The BYTR

My Next Encounter

With Sister having spiraled into her deadly abyss, I must move on. Yes, Sister is a sad story, from pairing an unsuspecting user with a BYTR.

As for me, I merely journey on to target my next user/victim.

I expect that next someone will also be as naïve as Sister. Maybe one of her co-workers or maybe one of *your* colleagues as the cycle repeats itself.

Maybe it will be *you*.

Sister's replacement now presents herself as someone ready for my next bite, someone unaware of my cunning, stealth, and deadly skills. Although I miss having that deep connection with Sister, I cannot wait for this new relationship, another target… another *luscious* target.

Bite… Bite… ***BYTE.***

A Powerful Secret Weapon
A BYTR FYTR

I now have to watch out for Sister's kid sibling Joy, who, because of my winning battle against Sister, found the means to do serious battle with me.

Joy gathered focus, with specialized education, inspiration, and professional training, she became, of all things, a real BYTR FYTR, a Credentialed Ergonomist.

Now an Ergonomist is one of those soldiers who I fear most. A good one has knowledge, weapons, and techniques with which to keep my malevolent skills in check. They learn what to do when they recognize the trail marks of the BYTRs.

Even to this moment, I remain wary of Joy's efforts to curtail my activities. She has become quite an adversary. We battle each other in gamesmanship. Sometimes I win, but mostly she wins. However, when I win, some users realize they can reach out to her for help and methods to combat me. She is now a valuable resource to those and her employer.

We have had many encounters, Joy and I. She knows what to do when my biting reveals itself. With her a large arsenal of weaponry, including an effective and proactive approach to stopping and keeping me at bay. With the ability and knowledge to stop me in my tracks, she has proven to be a formidable foe, capable of denying me access to any part of a target's anatomy.

But that matters not. If Joy can take care of the wrists, I do not worry. I move on and target another part of the body. Maybe the shoulders, or elbow, maybe even the back. That is until someone sharp like Joy comes around and *ruins* my fun. When Joy can fix one person, she moves onto another and fixes them, and so on and so on.

Me? I don't mind. Like Joy, I also move onto another target, someone who Joy cannot get to, in another cubicle, another department, another building, another state, another country. Fortunately for me, the competent *Joys* of the world are rare. If you know a Joy or one of her fellow soldiers, you would do well to cherish and keep them as part of your weaponry against the BYTR Collective.

For me? I have little trouble finding another victim who is as unaware as Sister once was. If I am fortunate, Joy or some other good Ergo-Soldier will not be within striking distance, and I can do what I do best… Bite.

A Final Note to Sister

Goodbye Sister, I'll miss our time together, I'll miss your admiration, I'll miss your touch, and I'll miss our adventures.

Just to let you know, your replacement also has a laptop she uses at home and is just as enthusiastic as you were. She's not as fast or as good or as smart as you, but I don't mind; she's an adequate replacement.

Just like you, I needn't set a trap for her. She visits me regularly, and, I have all the time in the world. Unfortunately, management provided her the identical workstation set-up you had. Now, it is only a matter of time. You understand do you not? I thought so...

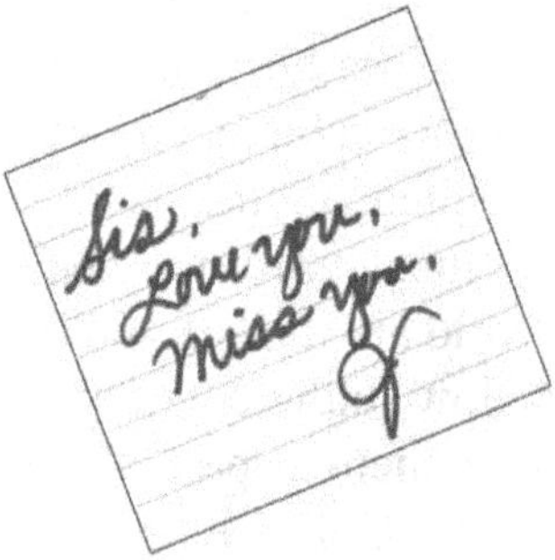

BYTR BIT

Consider few users have knowledge of methods to combat BYTR onslaughts.

Thus, users like Sister remain easy targets.

Non-acknowledgement enables free BYTR actions, especially with shoddy work performed by uninformed practitioners (See *Ergonomic Mis-Adventures, Chapter III, Snake-Oil Ergonomics*).

Seeking help?
Reference the BYTR FYTR Manual–Section III.

Section I

Endnote

Your Adversary Identified
Plus Another–DYVR

Your Adversary Identified

Having been introduced to a true demon, you now know this deadly thing means to do you much harm.

This being represents a target to whom you can aim your concern, your hatred, your efforts to quash preventing damage to your life's activities.

Like tennis, it is difficult to play if you cannot see your opponent. Although ethereal and invisible, you can still visualize this BYTR as a real entity, an enemy you must combat to save the only body you will ever have. It behooves you to identify how and where it attacks. You must challenge it, make plans and take action defending yourself against its destructive actions.

Remember, it is solely up to you to keep yourself whole, to take the BYTR Challenge and emerge victoriously (p. 137).

You must first understand yourself and those things that are specifically harmful to you as you use your computer devices.

Fear not — there exists much hope and many solutions for you.

Actions are necessary, to be taken for fully addressing the specific causes and relationships to your pain. Successful solutions are readily available in Section III.

However, an intimate sense of self-understanding must be generated before even the remotest chance of success can be secured.

You must know yourself to understand your body as the battlefield. Know the way you perform your computer tasking. Most of all understand your pain issues and use the knowledge in this tome to defend your health.

To successfully prepare yourself, follow this sage Human wisdom.

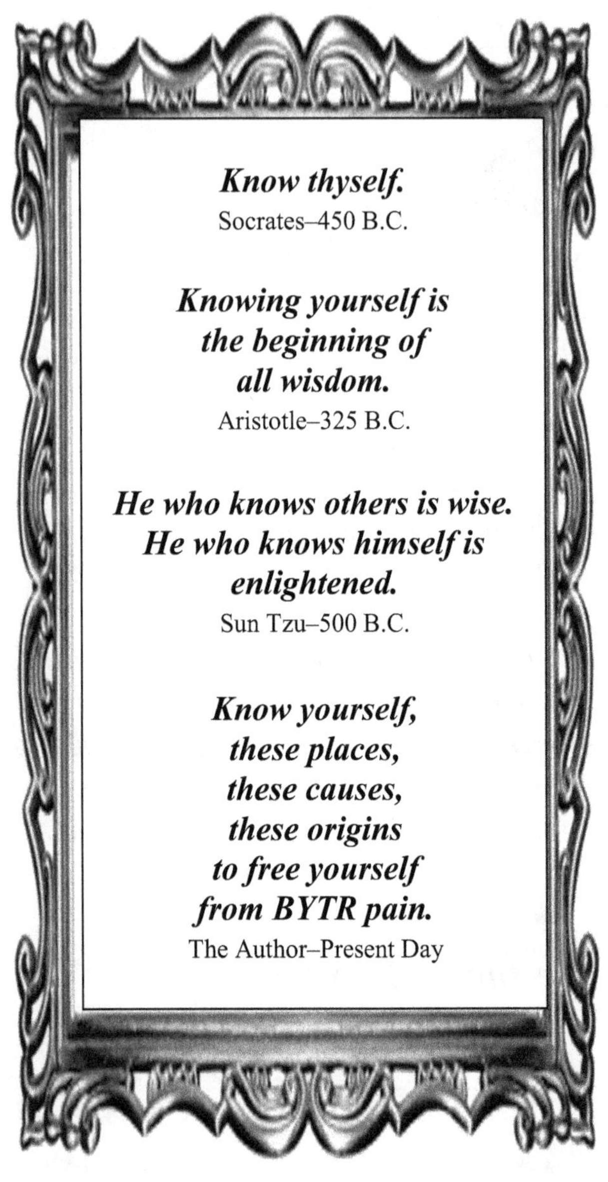

Know thyself.

Socrates–450 B.C.

Knowing yourself is
the beginning of
all wisdom.

Aristotle–325 B.C.

He who knows others is wise.
He who knows himself is
enlightened.

Sun Tzu–500 B.C.

Know yourself,
these places,
these causes,
these origins
to free yourself
from BYTR pain.

The Author–Present Day

Meet

BYTR'S Best Friend DYVR*

And DYVR's Nemesis

RYDR*

(one who can help you)

Know there are bites other than the physical wounds rendered onto your body. These manifest themselves in the way of stresses and expectations beyond yourself, touching your emotional core. Called psychological or mental strain, these also contribute highly to your downfall. Presented here is yet another means to wreck mayhem onto yourself.

*** Created by Dr. Lynn McAtamney** CPE APAM
Co-author RULA & REBA

Meet BYTR'S Best Friend DYVR

Another adversary who can bring you down

So… we meet. I am DYVR, pronounced 'Diver'. I am an entity lurking in a place deep within your psyche. I delight in dragging you down into hidden, private doubts, and fears. Most everyone has a vulnerability that opens to these-your painful depths.

Like BYTR, I am **in** you, I always have been, and always will be. However, unlike BYTR, I play in your mind finding your weaknesses, your places of vulnerability where I can open your thoughts and manipulate you. Creating frustration, anger, and dark moods are my calling. I invite you to apply these with the worst excesses of your hidden self to place yourself in a spiral going deeper and deeper.

I can be heard or be silent–that is up to you. DYVR's delight is in your falling, fading, and sinking–especially when it is from old habits and thoughts. You will be teased with self-doubt and with words of failure or inadequacy. I can even convince you as being insignificant.

Continually prowling, despising the light, preferring the shadows and darkness, I will fight hard to keep you there. DYVR methodically invites you down, and if not wary, can overtake you, just like BYTR.

DYVR Bio

Street Name

- DYVR–derived from a 13th-century term *Dufan* "to dive, duck, sink, to become submerged in a deep hollow"
- Pronounced 'Diver'

Physical Characteristics

- Innate/Invisible

Current Whereabouts

- Known to inhabit the human mind
- Attaches to human fear, doubt, failures, anxieties, addictions, and depression
- Able to enter Human psyche without warning

Associates/ Affiliates

- Known associate of BYTR
- Considered a member of The Collective

Victim Profile

- Random unsuspecting computer users
- No distinguishable age, gender or social group
- Infiltrates human life even when device usage ends

Caution/ Warning

- Highly active
- ***Considered highly destructive to Human behavior***

Most Effective Defense

- Proactive prevention with patience, application, awareness
- Consult RESILIENCE Manual (soon available)

Meet RYDR (DYVR's nemesis)

One who can help you

My name is RYDR, pronounced RIDER. I am an actual psychological attribute within you; some call it your soul or spirit, values or drive. You recognize me when you feel the sense of accomplishment at something you did not think you could complete, or stepping through a difficult situation with a sense of peace and success amidst the challenges.

I am a colleague of FYTR–building your body, mind, and soul into a strong place to defend you from DYVR and BYTR. I can guide and encourage you to places of thriving, hope and fulfillment-but only if you allow me. My desire is that you are equipped to ride the rough waves and challenges in life, and not be taken in or down by my adversary, DYVR.

You need no translation as to DYVR's motives, but just to declare his presence helps to fight him. DYVR talks with a silver tongue, and sometimes more loudly than me, so you may know and feel him first. But I am with you and always will be, waiting to be invited in.

As you read this, you may hear DYVR telling you this is rubbish, or reminding you of something you should do instead. Maybe DYVR is only performing actions to pull you down.

I am here to equip you with tools to fight stress, failure or frustrations. I will help you find peace, courage, energy, to know you are valued. All you require is to seek me out, and I will help guide you through the challenges. You need only ask.

RYDR Bio

Street Name

- RYDR–derived from old English word "rīdere" meaning "a mounted warrior–one who rises above and conquers"
- Pronounced Rider.

Physical Characteristics

- Innate/Invisible
- Patient, empathetic, ethical

Current Whereabouts

- Known to inhabit any Human mind
- Available at any time on request
- Present in every Human
- Silent if not recognized, not valued or not listening

Associates/Affiliates

- Known Associate of BYTR FYTR

Host Profile

- Resides in all Human minds
- No distinguishable age, gender or social group
- Easily seen in children before life experiences cloud their minds, behaviors, and decisions

Areas Most Effective

- Guidance through challenging times
- Enabling choices in change
- Works with Peace, Action, Courage, and Energy
- Enabling choices in reacting and behavior
- Finding meaning and contentment in life

RYDR Weapons: Resilience & PACE

DYVR and RYDR journey with you through life's realities and challenges, providing honest reflections involving work, home, and relationship truths. You will find familiar thoughts and habits. Many will please you. Some will not, revealing gaps in your life.

DYVR has a sharp tongue and keen insight into your vulnerabilities, and together with BYTR create pain and distraction. RYDR cuts through these destructive temptations providing a guiding light on new paths and choices.

Beware how DYVR will pull you down with deceitful negative chatter, desires for perfection and needs to delay choices through doubts or subtle fears. DYVR circles and loves distracting you, creating disharmony and feeding on unhealthy habits. Your journey is ultimately about Resilience, a process to enhance your ability to rise up and successfully meet challenges or adversity, presented in four life areas (P.A.C.E.).

- Peace (how to get and keep it)
- Action (time-saving and time-wasting)
- Courage (for challenging times)
- Energy (keeping your engine fueled)

PACE meets you at the place you are now and takes you where DYVR no longer drags on your life, providing a resource for you to graze and to dip into as needed.

You will learn to know yourself better. Each of us has within ourselves dark reactions to pressures revealing themselves when your resilience is slipping.

RYDR Weapons: Resilience & PACE

A desire to journey to a place for honest reflection and focus on balancing your internal Resilience with life demands?

RYDR can guide you to these places where your body, mind, and soul are well.

You are quite unique; as is your journey.

RYDR Remark

While BYTR lays siege to your physical being, your allies are the BYTR FYTRS.

While DYVR attacks your psyche and your soul, I am at your side, your companion and confidant, at the ready to help you through those dark professional and personal times. You have but to ask.

Check the BYTR Blog for the launch date of RYDR's Resilience and PACE.

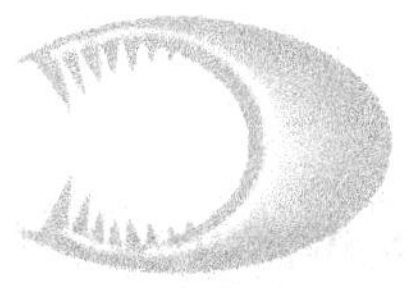

Beware The BYTR!

SECTION II

The Reality of Your Pain

The pain, injury, and causations in this section are real and non-fiction... the facts in this section are also real and non-fiction.

Use this information to understand the attacks on your body and livelihood , and to develope a plan to combat these insidious demons and your own injury-causing actions.

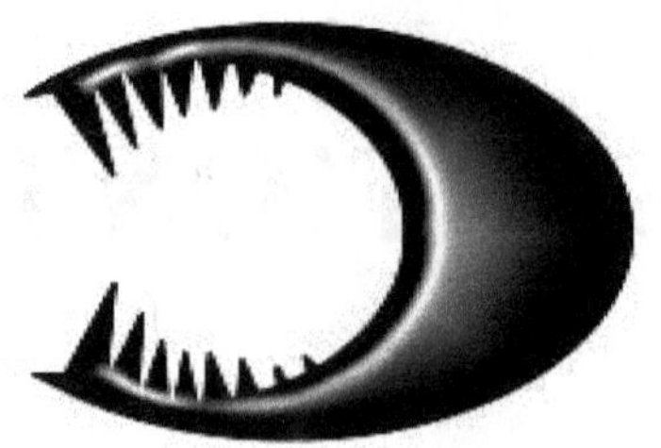

Introduction–You are in Peril!

Can you imagine losing the use of your hands? Can you imagine your ability to pick up your infant children taken away from you?

Can you imagine not being able to perform personal or professional tasks such as holding a fork or keyboarding? Can you imagine your inability to perform self-care or to provide for your family due to wracking pain in your hands, wrists, arms, or legs?

Can you conceive of not being able to stand up, sit or walk for more than a few minutes from the stabbing back pain or shocks shooting down your legs?

These are the realities and results of injuries from intensive computer usage as you let the BYTRS run wild. It might be you, someone you know or someone you love. Frightening.

The Reality of Your Pain

Section II

Table of Contents

ADDENDUM to Section II

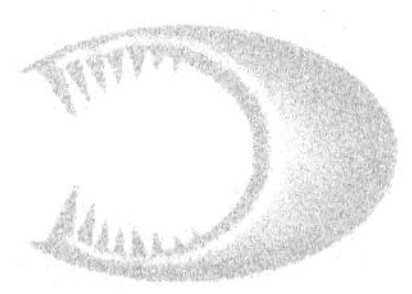

Beware The BYTR!

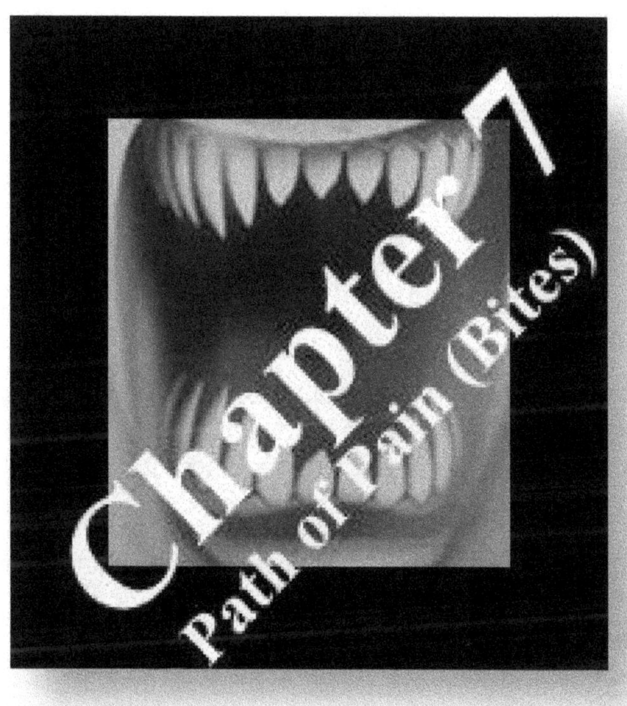

Real World Specifics

Chapter 7

THE PATH OF THE PAIN (BITES)

HOW IS YOUR BODY ATTACKED?

Biting affects mostly the primary intimate contact point between us: your hands. Thumbs and necks of small device users also are intensely at risk.

Understand, The BYTR Easily Moves Throughout Your Body from One Area to Another.

Biting on your wrists prompts carpal tunnel syndrome or tendinitis. Next, is maneuvering to the hands triggering ache. From there it's onto your fingers imparting numbness or tingling.

If you or your BYTR FYTR reduces this hand symptomology, BYTR will forage at your elbow inciting epicondylitis. Then it moves up to your shoulder to instigate bicipital groove inflammation.

Another target is the neck with migraine-inducing muscle tightness or nerve compression. Onward to the mid-back, the shoulder blades, low back, then onto the hips, legs, and feet.

The BYTR Collective has total access to your entire body.

Witness this path of Bites.

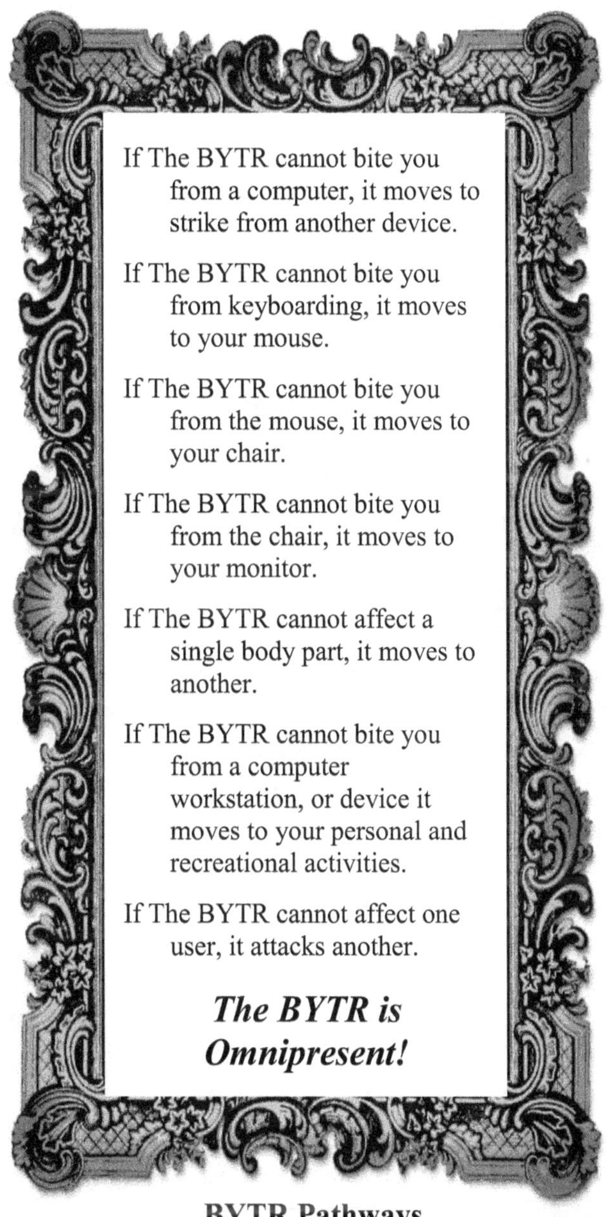

If The BYTR cannot bite you from a computer, it moves to strike from another device.
If The BYTR cannot bite you from keyboarding, it moves to your mouse.
If The BYTR cannot bite you from the mouse, it moves to your chair.
If The BYTR cannot bite you from the chair, it moves to your monitor.
If The BYTR cannot affect a single body part, it moves to another.
If The BYTR cannot bite you from a computer workstation, or device it moves to your personal and recreational activities.
If The BYTR cannot affect one user, it attacks another.
The BYTR is Omnipresent!

BYTR Pathways

BYTR movements throughout your anatomy are continual and unencumbered:

No matter what activity is performed,
No matter how it is performed,
No matter where it is performed,
No matter when it is performed,

Every biomechanical element combined with repetitive or at-risk movement and posture, provides open invitations and targets for bite placement.

Any repetitive, forceful or at-risk motion is a potential hazard or pain trigger, whether using a computer device or perform any professional, personal or recreational task, using any professional, personal or recreational tool.

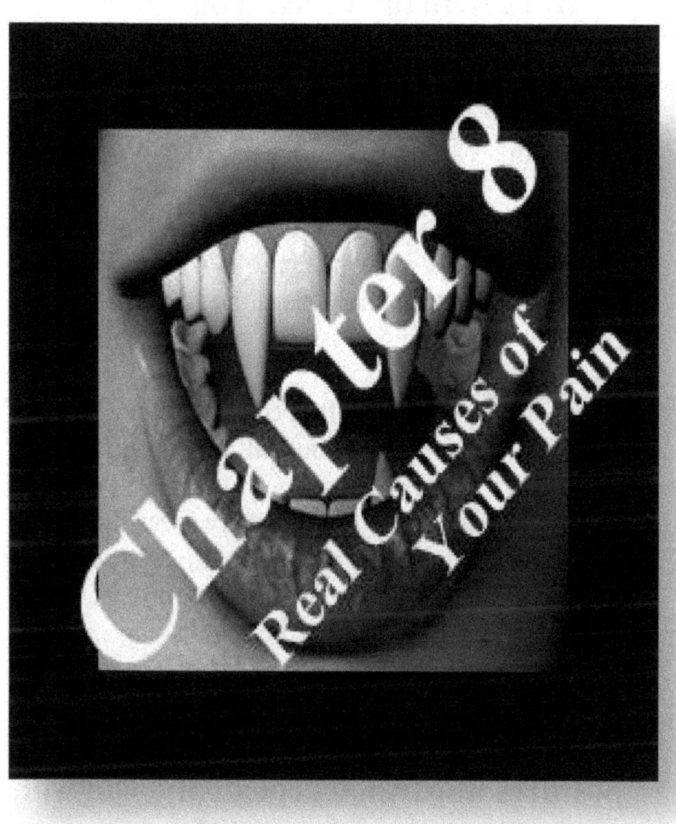
Chapter 8
Real Causes of
Your Pain

The Definitive Revealing List of Where Bites Actually Cause Your Pain*

Here are reality checklists and diagrams to help identify the specific tasks and motions triggering your pain.

Use these roadmaps to familiarize yourself with exact body areas susceptible to BYTR pain and how discomfort occurs. Learn the motions and postures that are the base root cause of your pain.

Some are very subtle, often overlooked because of this. Some are very obvious, all are important.

Offer attention to the high priority areas that are painful or showing even minimal discomfort. Then you can develop a proactive approach against The BYTR Collective.

If you DO NOT perform the adverse postures illustrated repeatedly, you will prevent or lessen your pain!

Some pain is easily reduced by simple postural or action changes. An experienced BYTR FYTR can help here. Some users may need specific equipment applications described in the BYTR FYTR Field Manual, Section III.

Common Mousing & Keyboarding Pain Postures

When Mousing or Keyboarding
"Don't Wave Hello or Goodbye."

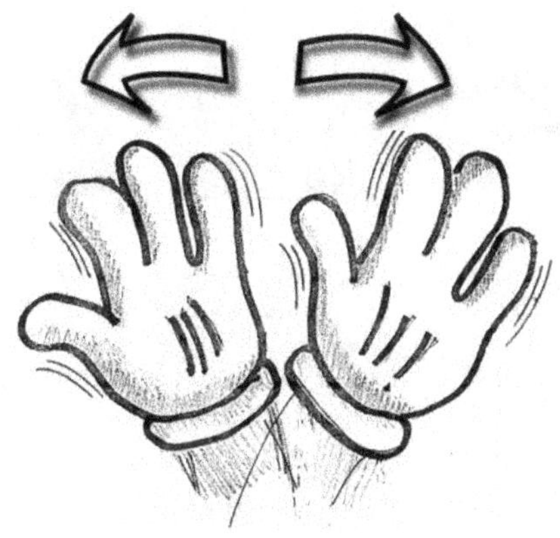

No waving ***Hello***
Rapid Back & forth–radial & ulnar deviation

No waving ***Goodbye***
Rapid Up & Down–flexion and extension

Common Mousing & Keyboarding Pain Postures

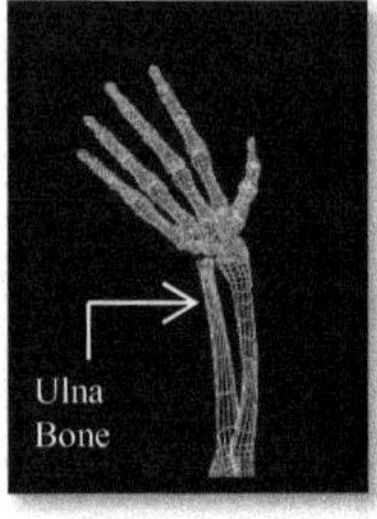

Ulnar Deviation*–
Hand bent towards
ulna bone

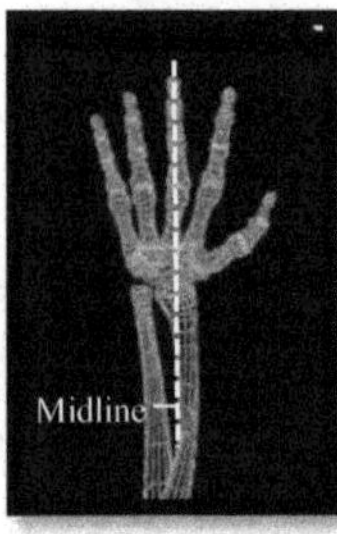

Preferred Body-
Neutral*
No bending

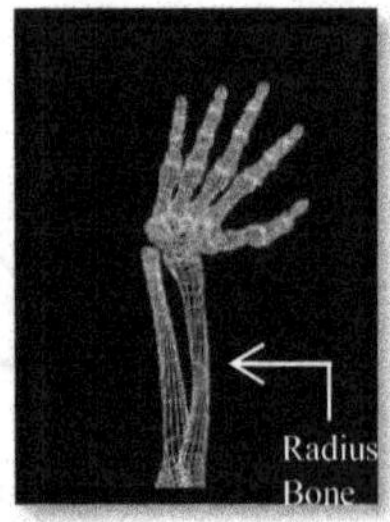

Radial Deviation*-
Hand bent towards
radius bone

Hand Radial & Ulnar Deviation* angled away from the midline
The basic cause of carpal tunnel syndrome and assorted pain
Don't hold your mouse or keyboard like this

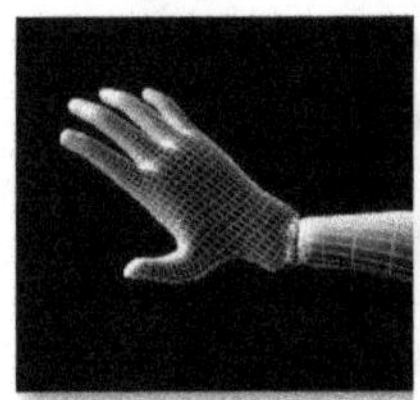

Extension
Bending hand upwards

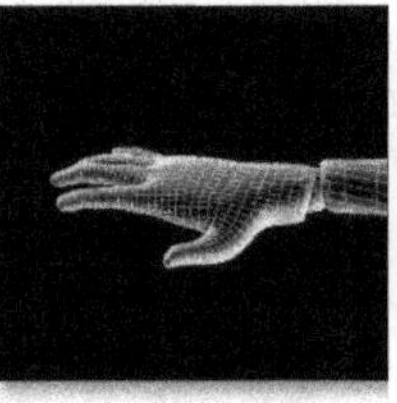

Body-Neutral
No bending

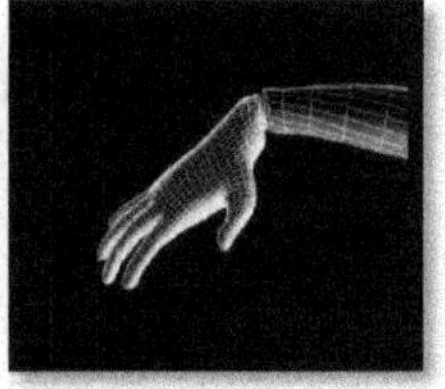

Flexion
Bending hand
downwards

Hand Flexion & Extension* angled away from the midline
Don't hold your mouse or work on your keyboard like this
This is the basic cause of carpal tunnel syndrome

* For understandable definitions, see BYTR Buzzwords
Section II Addendum–p.127

Common Mousing & Keyboarding Pain Postures

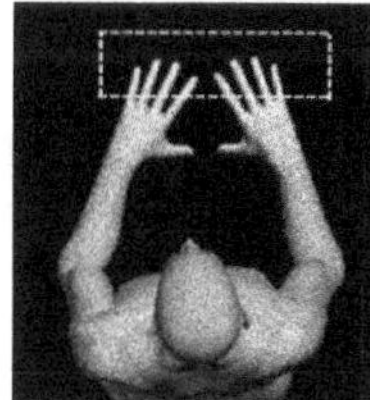

Inward arm rotation* with a typical keyboard

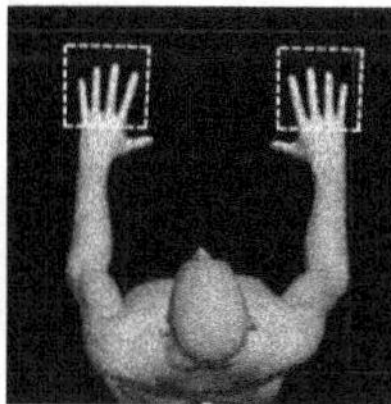

Preferred Body-Neutral* with split keyboard

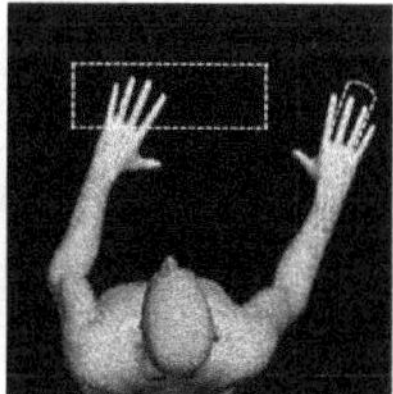

Inward rotation (left-hand) and outward rotation (right-hand) with typical keyboard & mouse

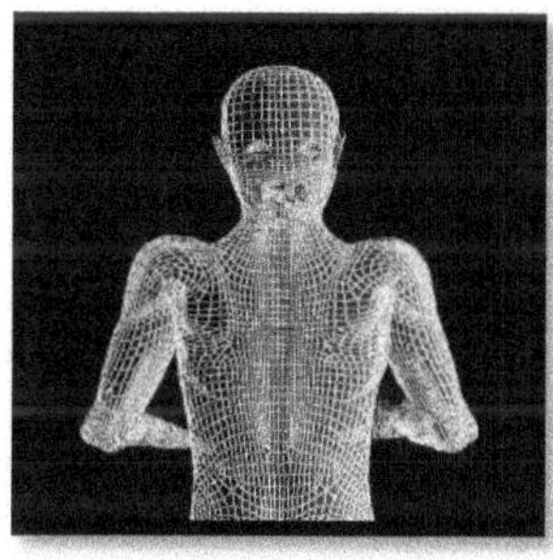

Raised shoulders with arms/elbows abducted*– standing or sitting with hands on a high desk, keyboard, mouse or chair arms

Raised shoulders with arms/elbows abducted*– standing or sitting with hands on keyboard or mouse

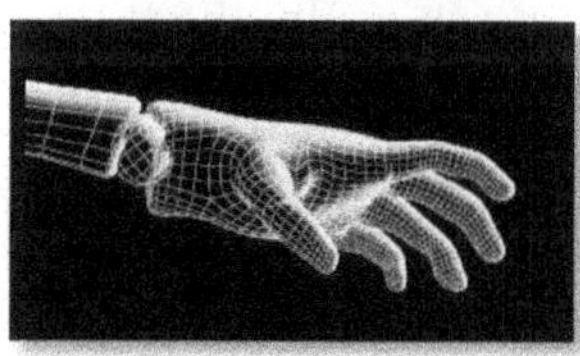

Pronation–twisting to palm down position for keyboard access

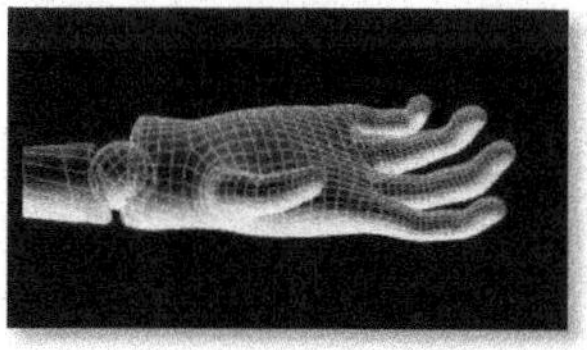

Supination–palm up "Asking for soup"

* For understandable definitions, see BYTR Buzzwords–p.129

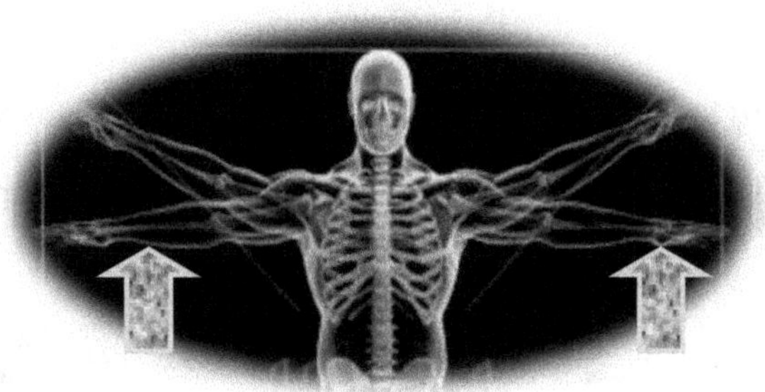

Wrist Bites / Pain

Caused By:

- ☐ Highly repetitive keyboarding–(finger action while the hand is in ulnar deviation/bent outwards)
- ☐ Highly repetitive mousing (hand action moving left to right/ulnar & radial deviation)
- ☐ Holding fingers too tightly on a mouse–(Tension on tendons passing through the carpal tunnel in wrist causing swelling and irritation, aka CTS)
- ☐ Bad positioning on a keyboard in both flexion and extension–(constantly having wrists bent upwards in extension, with or without a wrist support or using an improper one)
- ☐ Resting forearms/wrists on front sharp desk edge–(contact or impact stress)
- ☐ Pressing <enter> or <backspace> keys simultaneously especially with ulnar deviated wrists (right hand turned outwards)

Wrist Bites / Pain–con't

- Pressing <esc> or <tab> keys especially with ulnar deviated wrists (left-hand turned outwards)
- Everyday office equipment. i.e. 3-hole paper punch, pincher staple remover, and rubber bands–inherent actions and typical office tasks causing hand, finger, wrist and elbow pain–see Desktop Tool Pain Generation in The BYTR FYTR manual, Section III)

Typical "claw" finger posture stressing tendons passing through the carpal tunnel (syndrome)

Bent wrists, crushing carpal tunnel at the underside of the wrist by resting on the sharp desk edge is an invitation for BYTR attacks

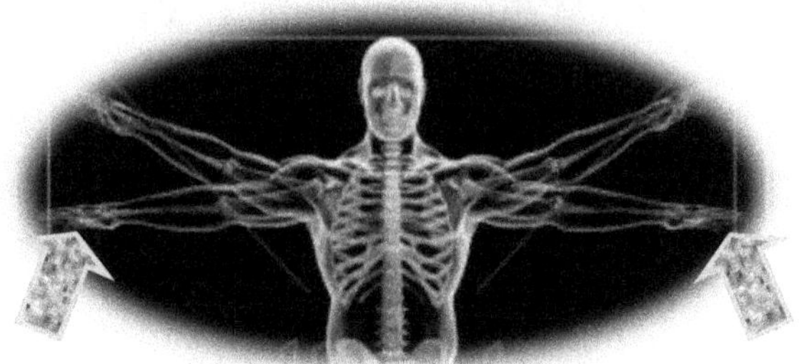

Hands & Finger Bites / Pain
Caused By:

- ☐ Bending fingers into “claw” positions on keyboard home rows–(muscle tension & fatigue)
- ☐ Squeezing mouse with “death grips” between thumb and small fingers-(muscle tension & fatigue)
- ☐ Tightly holding game controllers
- ☐ Squeezing or holding pens too tightly
- ☐ Squeezing or holding the computer stylus too tightly
- ☐ Texting with thumbs while holding cell phones with fingers in tensioned “claw” position
- ☐ Tightly held fingers holding computer tablets (static loading without relief)
- ☐ Pressing <enter>or <backspace> keys especially with ulnar deviated wrists (right-hand turned outwards)
- ☐ Pressing <esc> or <tab> keys especially with ulnar deviated wrists (left hand turned outwards)

Hand & Finger Bites / Pain–con't

- Everyday office equipment. i.e. 3-hole paper punch, pincher staple remover and rubber bands–(see Desktop Tool Pain, p.265)

Stressed finger posture affecting hand and finger musculature and tendons passing through the carpal tunnel

Fingers held in "claw" position

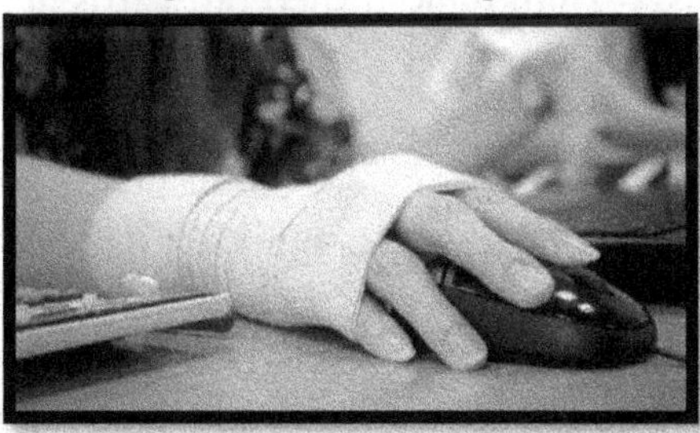

Damage from mouse "death" grip

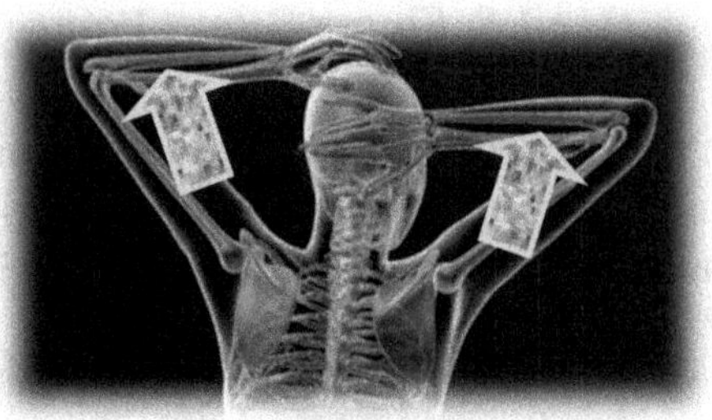

Forearm Bites / Pain
Caused By:

- Holding hands to a flat palm down positioning (pronation) at home row position (muscle strain)
- Holding arms up and outstretched to a high keyboard–on the desktop (muscle strain)
- Holding arms up and outstretched to a high mouse (on the desktop) or too far to the left or right (strain)
- Squeezing mouse with "death grips" between thumb and small fingers–(activates ongoing forearm muscle tension)
- Pressing <enter> or <backspace> keys simultaneously especially with ulnar deviated wrists- right hand turned outwards activating forearm musculature (static loading/muscle strain)
- Pressing <esc> or <tab> keys, especially with ulnar deviated wrists with left hand turned outwards activating forearm musculature (static loading, muscle strain)

Forearm Bites / Pain–con't

- Everyday office equipment. i.e.3-hole paper punch, pincher staple remover and rubber bands–(see Desktop Tool Pain, p.265)

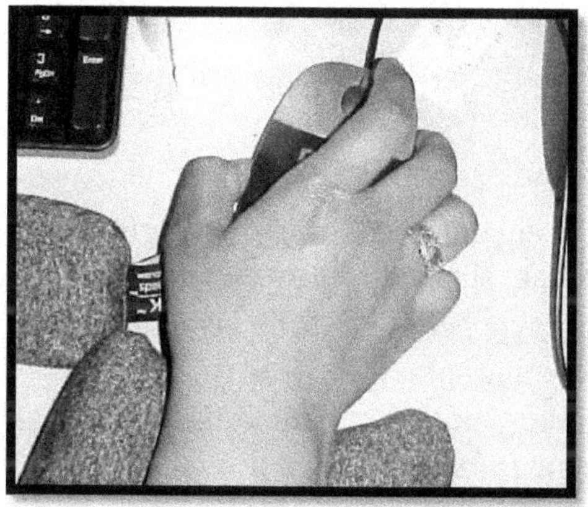

Squeezing mouse with "death grip" and ulnar deviation overuses and stresses forearm musculature

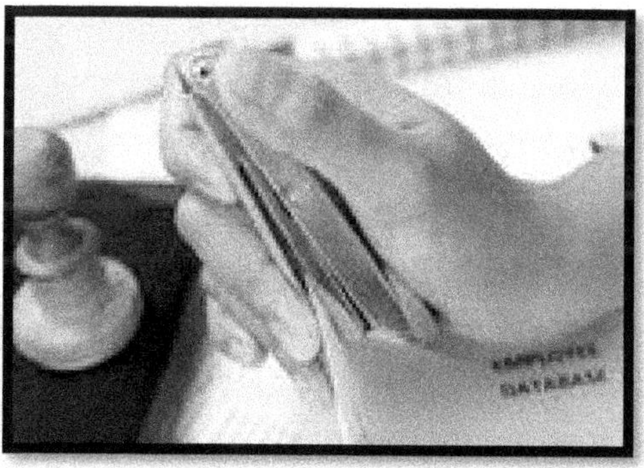

Forearm pain can be caused by severe repetitive gripping of office tools

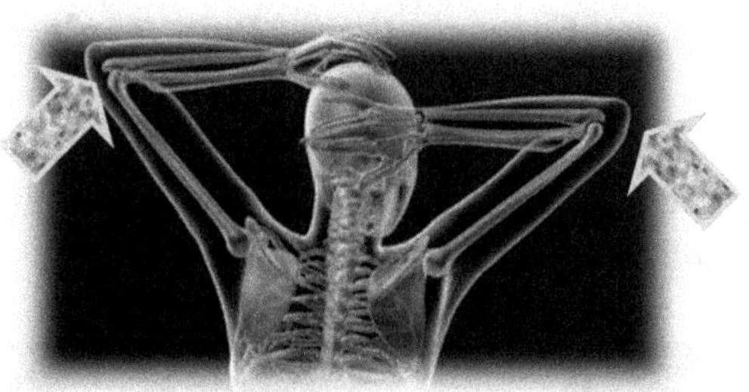

Elbow Bites / Pain
Caused By:

- ☐ Banging elbows against chair armrests (contact stress, bruising, sores, blood clots)
- ☐ Hovering hands over the keyboard (ulnar nerve entrapment)
- ☐ Holding elbows outside or inside of high chair armrests (ache from continual adverse positioning)
- ☐ Holding hands to a flat palm down positioning (pronation) during keyboarding–also tends to move elbows to an outboard position away from torso (arm abduction)
- ☐ Holding arms up and extended to a keyboard on a high desktop (places torsion on elbow)
- ☐ Holding arms up and outstretched to a high mouse on a desktop (places torsion on elbow held in position in front of and away from torso)
- ☐ Outward rotation to reach mouse too far to the left or right (holding arm out in space/lateral epicondylitis)

Elbow Bites / Pain–con't

- ☐ Squeezing mouse with "death grips" between thumb and small fingers directly forces continual forearm/elbow muscle tension

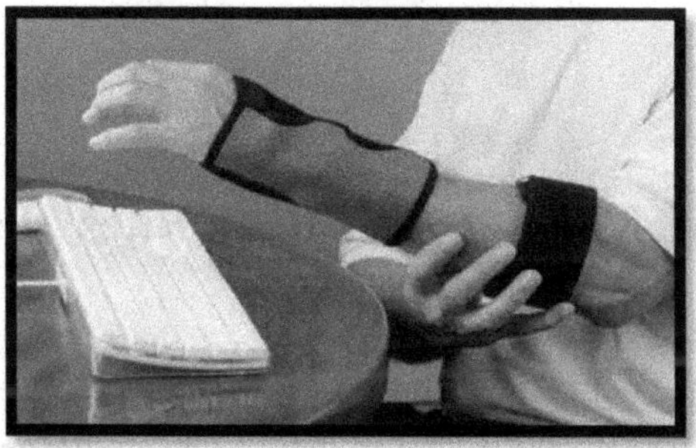

Forearm musculature, when pulled away from the lateral epicondyle (elbow), results in lateral epicondylitis

The continual banging of elbows against chair armrests invites cubital tunnel syndrome, shoulder pain, lateral epicondylitis, and medial epicondylitis among other maladies

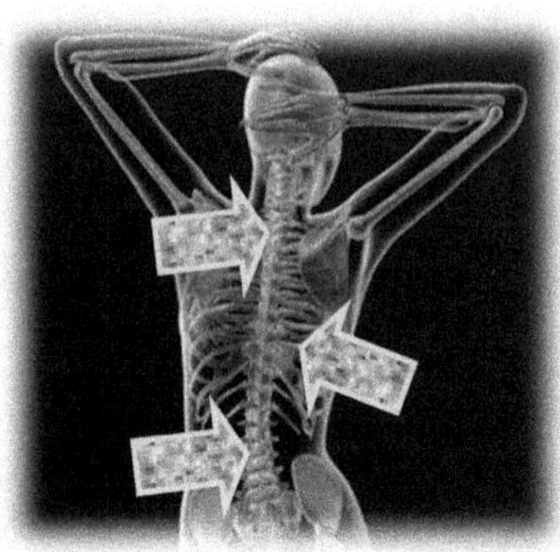

Low, Mid & Upper Back Bites / Pain
Caused By:

- ☐ Forward lean to view monitor (stressed, strained neck and upper back musculature from the extended head)
- ☐ Forward lean with seat pan too deep & without any back support (stressed, strained neck and upper back musculature from the extended head)
- ☐ Forward curvature of the entire back (total kyphosis stress and straining all large and small back musculature with static loading)
- ☐ Lack of low back lumbar curve (flattens out lumbar curve causing stress to low back musculature also resulting in pinching sciatic nerve, i.e. sciatica)
- ☐ Knee position too high forcing pelvic tilt (flattens out lumbar curvature and adversely tilts pelvis with more lumbar curve flattening –see above)
- ☐ Belt digging into the low back (into sciatic nerves)

Back Bites / Pain–con't

- ☐ Chair seat too deep (forces forward lean without adequate back support–see above)
- ☐ Chair seat too soft (compresses muscles and neural tracks at the back of thigh and buttocks with irritation)
- ☐ Chair seat too hard (point pressure on ischial tuberosities, aka "sit bones"–those hard bones in the middle of your derrière)

Extreme curvature of upper back from forced forward lean on high desktop affecting backs and necks

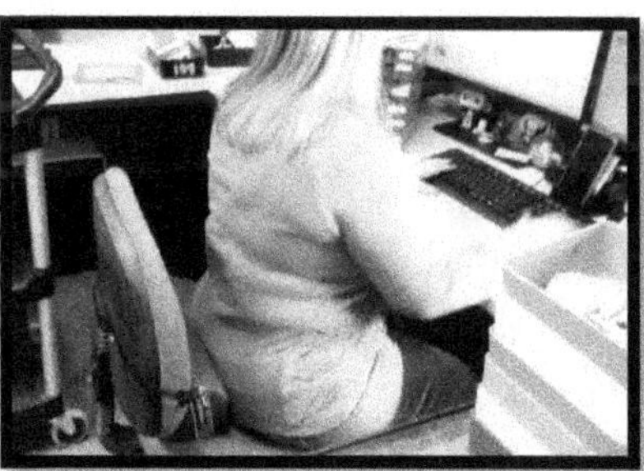

Unsupported back with ineffective lumbar cushion resulting in static loading of entire back musculature

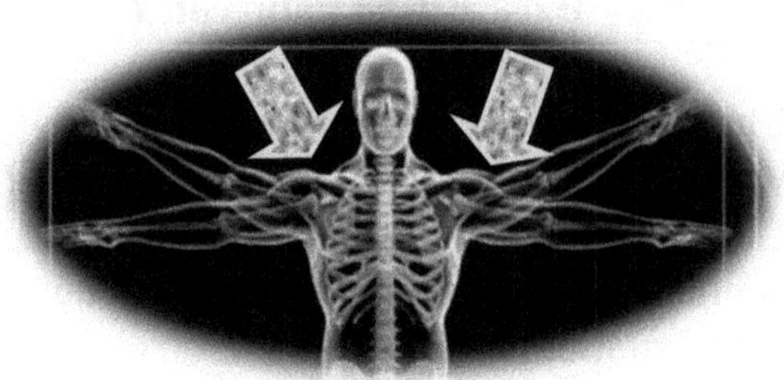

Shoulder Bites / Pain

Caused By:

- ☐ Outstretched arm to reach the keyboard or/mouse on a high desktop (static loading straining shoulder muscles)
- ☐ Outstretched arms to reach mouse on a high desktop (see above)
- ☐ Forward lean to view monitor too far away (inadvertent inward shoulder rotation or moving shoulders forward ahead of the neckline)
- ☐ Chair armrests too high or too low (raising shoulders well above natural hang with static loading)
- ☐ Chair armrests too wide or too narrow (constantly holding elbows away from torso with static loading)
- ☐ Leaning on elbows at extreme lateral lean, raising shoulders (pushes leaning shoulder above natural hang with shearing action at shoulder girdle)

Shoulder Bites / Pains– con't

- Clamping phone handset between head and shoulder (forces constant shoulder raising and head lateral flexion, compressing shoulder musculature & neural networks)
- Inward rotation of shoulders (habitual position straining shoulder musculature and compressing chest structures/rib cage)
- Holding arm up on high desktop (places torsion on shoulder girdle with static loading on extended arm held in position in front of and away from torso)
- Outstretched arm to reach the keyboard or/mouse on a high desktop (static loading straining shoulder muscles)

Entire forearm on high desktop forces continual shoulder raising and resultant shear forces– mousing hand is also rotated outward placing continual stressors on the shoulder

Raised shoulder by resting arm on a high desktop during keyboarding placing shear forces on the shoulder girdle

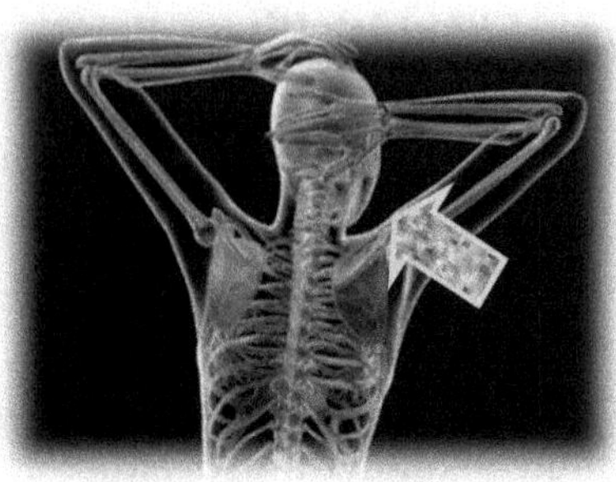

Neck Bites / Pain

Caused By: (not vampires)

- ☐ Bending neck to read reference material on flat desktops or on laptop screens
- ☐ Continual bent head when viewing cell phone held close to the chest or placed on a table
- ☐ Raising head to look at screens through the lower half of bifocal eyeglasses
- ☐ Leaning and moving head closer to screens for better monitor viewing
- ☐ Hunching or raising shoulders–habitual or stress-induced shoulder hunching
- ☐ Inward rotation of shoulders (also habitual or stress-induced)
- ☐ Improper prescription eyeglasses forcing forward lean or head tilt

All have significant casual relationships to the stress and strain of the upper back, upper shoulder, and neck musculature resulting in continued static loading with associated moderate to high pain levels.

Neck Bites / Pain–con't

- ☐ Stressed & tight shoulder and upper back musculature from unknown personal causes
- ☐ Inadequate backrest support affecting upper back musculature

Extreme head pulled to forward position taxes neck & upper back musculature–a major cause of neck and shoulder pain

Head forward past midline and chin pushed forward to closely view monitor in focal plane effects neck pain

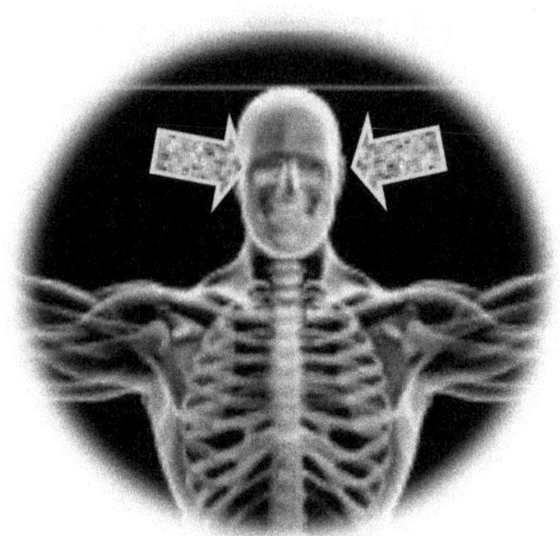

Eye Bites / Pain
Caused By:

- ☐ Prolonged viewing of monitor screens (especially under the following conditions)
- ☐ Excessively bright ambient/background light
- ☐ Bright sunlight close to sightlines or on the monitor screen (monitor facing a window)
- ☐ Poor monitor contrast
- ☐ Small screen print
- ☐ Inappropriate (glaring, bright) monitor colors
- ☐ Small on-screen visual objects
- ☐ Overhead lighting glare–into the face or onto the screen (wash)
- ☐ Lack of opportunity to focus on distant objects
- ☐ Improper/ inadequate corrective lenses/contacts (not dedicated "computer eyeglasses/lenses")
- ☐ Prolonged wearing of contact lenses without hydration or refreshing moisture
- ☐ Airflow causing surface irritation or "dry eye"

Eye Bites / Pain–con't

The focal plane is incorrect; compounded with improper (prescription) eyeglasses, forcing the head into a forward position for monitor viewing

AUTHOR'S note

Burning, drying, and itching eyes; along with blurred vision, or inability to focus often result from overuse and strain of the tiny eye muscles

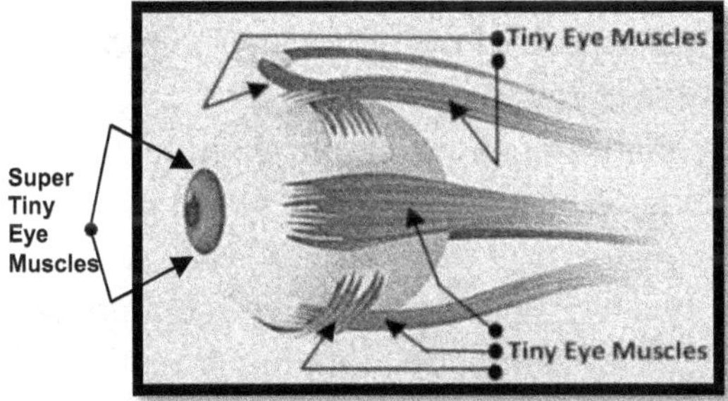

Super tiny muscles inside the eye, circle and manipulate the shape of the lens and pupil opening-other tiny muscles (like small rubber bands) spin the eyeball around on three axes, and like other muscles, fatigue with overuse or static loading causing pain and discomfort, AKA eye strain

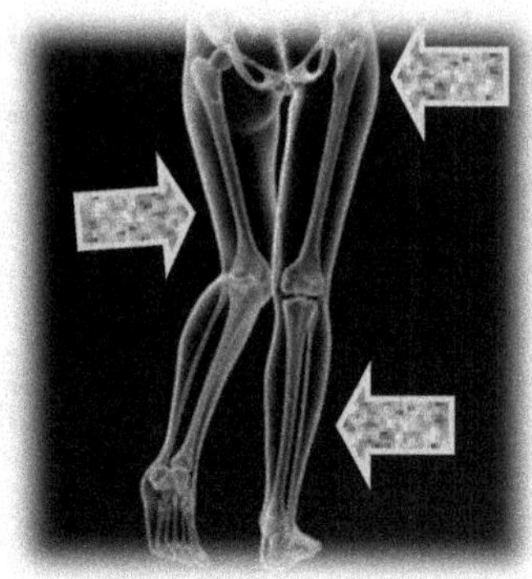

Leg Bites / Pain

Caused By:

- ☐ Seated position with knees higher than hips closing up the angle between torso and leg-stretching sciatic neural tracks and compressing vasculature (numbness & tingling)
- ☐ High chair seat crushing vasculature and neural tracks behind the knee (popliteal crease) and back of the upper leg (pain & numbness in lower leg & foot)
- ☐ Deep chair seat pan forcing forward lean stretching sciatic nerve around buttocks (sciatica)
- ☐ Prolonged sitting compressing vasculature & neural tracks numbness, tingling & pain in legs, feet, ankles and toes)
- ☐ Phones and wallets in back pockets crushing vasculature and neural tracks behind thighs and through the lower back (pinching sciatic nerve tracks with pain, numbness & tingling in legs, feet, and toes)

Leg Bites / Pain–con't

- Too low a chair bringing the knees above the hip (forcing pelvic tilt and flattens the lumbar curve, see above)
- Too low a keyboard or laptop forcing forward lean (flattening the lumbar curve, with pelvic tilt, see above)
- Footrests elevating knees closing torso/leg angle (see above)
- Belt digging into the back (see above)

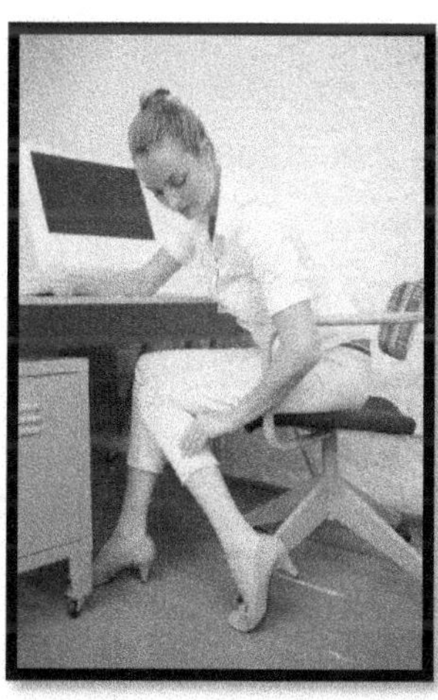

Improper shoes, footrest, desktop height, or chair seat heights will trigger leg and ankle pain

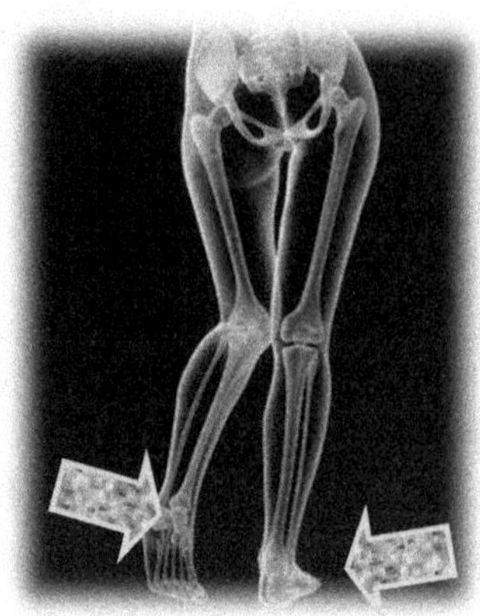

Foot & Ankle Bites / Pain

Caused By:

- ☐ Continuous flexed foot
- ☐ Chair too high
- ☐ Feet placed back on chair star base
- ☐ Knees too high
- ☐ Stretched leg
- ☐ Wastebasket in the way-causing body twist
- ☐ Bad shoes placing harmful pressure on feet
- ☐ Use of an improper footrest
- ☐ Not using a footrest when needed
- ☐ No movement of feet when locked on a footrest
- ☐ Continuous foot flexion or extension on edge of a flat footrest, chair foot rail, or starbase casters
- ☐ Improper floor mat during standing position
- ☐ Static loading–insufficient movement or stretching affecting pre-existing conditions such as varicose veins

Foot & Ankle Bites / Pain–con't

Improper chair or adjustments, shoes, and sitting posture contribute to foot & ankle pain

Care should be taken with appropriate application as improper footrests can produce severe foot or ankle pain

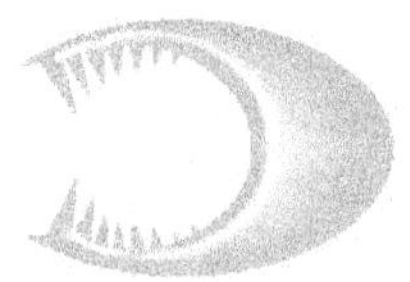

Beware The BYTR!

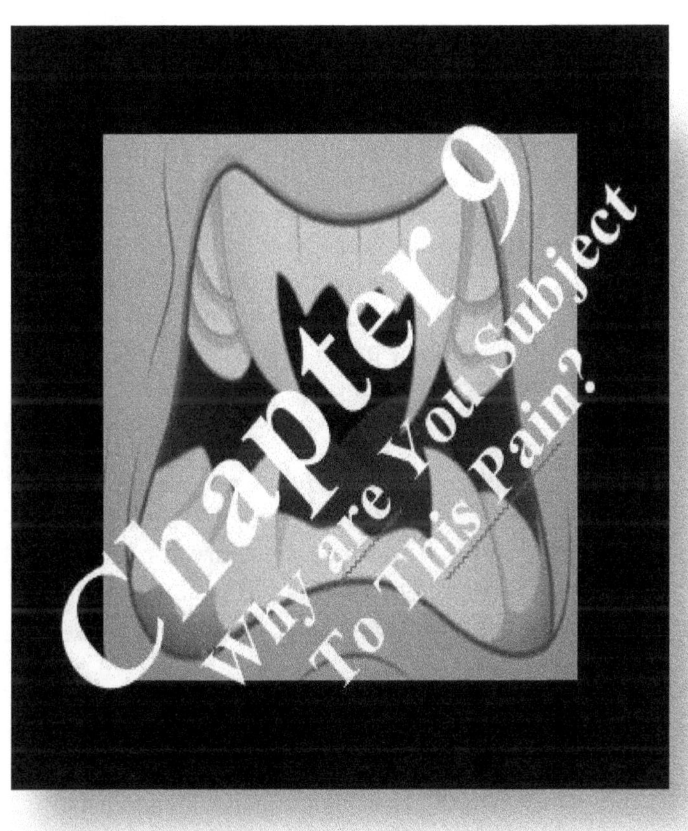
Chapter 9
Why are You Subject
To This Pain?

More Real World Specifics

Your Pain Contributors

I. ***The relationship of how much you and BYTR interface.***
The more you work or play together, the more biting opportunities. Every power user will eventually succumb at some level.

II. ***Inherited traits and genetics.***
Does injury or pain come easily? Have your forefathers contributed to your level of vulnerability by withholding the gift of the physical fortitude to withstand a BYTR onslaught?

III. ***Immediate health and current body condition.***
Is your body strong enough to prevent invasion? An illness or injury or not maintaining a state of physical well-being, will provide open invitations for… Bites.

IV. ***The Ergonomics of your workstation.***
Are the applications of workstation elements or tools correct or ineffective, specific to your body or your tasks?

V. ***Current bite level from workstations and personal activity.***
Are current injuries easily worsened?

VI. ***Age.***
Is your body ready to succumb from all previous work, pleasure or other contributory life activities?

"Why Do I Hurt?" "Why Me?" You Say, "Why, Why, WHY?"

You see, that very first bite began a steadily growing pain process. Slowly at first, building and escalating, setting fire to your wrists, numbing your fingers, or inserting a knife into your back. You don't know why, only being aware of the hurt, of your pain threshold reaching its limits. Until now, you have mostly pushed through the discomfort.

You feel that it really isn't anything serious and given time it should just sort itself out.

Old adages still ring in your head.

"No pain, no gain!"

"No one ever said work was easy!"

"It's just for a few minutes, and I'll be fine!"

Years of falsehood preaching and embedded deep in your psyche (ref. DYVR, p.69), these mantras direct your actions, and subconsciously you listen to them, ignoring the real causes. Confused, by not understanding, or rather (subconsciously) ignoring the logical pain sequence, you often look in wrong places for (quick) answers.

"Why Am I So Susceptible?"

You know trauma is not the root cause of your pain. No car accident or whiplash. So why *does* your neck hurt? You didn't fall down during that rec-league soccer game, so why does your shoulder ache?

It can't possibly be the computer, now can it? Maybe it's just old age: everyone gets aches and pain, do they not?

Candidly, your anatomy cannot withstand computing tasks. You are not cut out for this and shouldn't be doing it. Comparable to football team tryouts, mental fortitude and desire may exist, but physical attributes are severely lacking. By not being big enough, fast enough, or strong enough, your body is completely unsuited for the hitting, tackling, and violent contact. Similarly, it cannot handle intense keyboarding, mousing or any other power computer tasking.

Your anatomy is that which is quickly affected by bites, equal to an immediate, intense allergic reaction.

Like that allergic reaction, with its presence unknown until that first horrible outbreak, biting injuries can be similar. This sensitivity level is unknown until reacting to a real bout of intense input tasking.

Everyone gets bitten at some time, at some level…

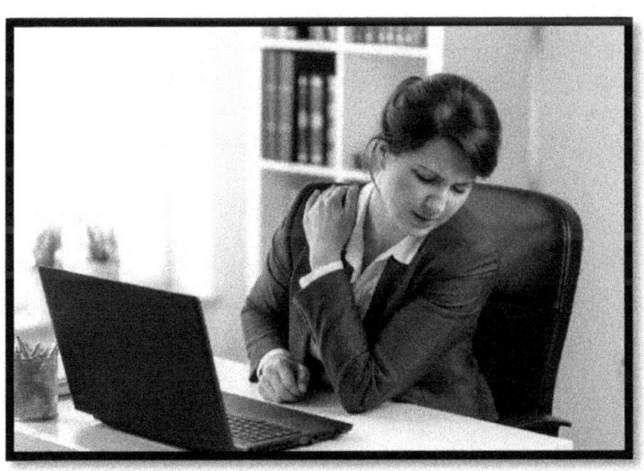

…No matter who you are.

Solutions documented in The BYTR FYTR Field Manual, Section III.

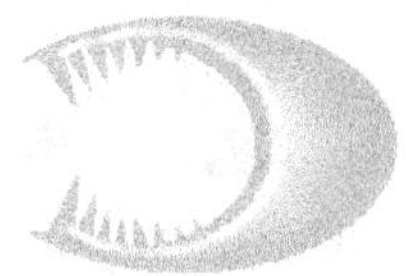

Beware The BYTR!

Chapter 10

False and Fake Solutions Thrive

Beware of the “Snake Oil”

False Solutions (things labeled "Ergonomic" but in actuality, are not

Be cautious! For many "Ergonomic" things provide false hopes of a *"magical"* cure. Such belief borders on complete fantasy and only result in endless loops of costly failure (See following and Section III for Voodoo Ergonomics Catalog).

Many users too often think a solution is to obtain a device advertised, touted or labeled as "Ergonomic," only to discover ineffective outcomes, increasing pain and high frustration.

Suggestions from friends, co-workers and equipment vendors although well-intentioned, often provide improper devices or information, often making pain or injury worse. Inappropriate application or vast misunderstanding of causal relationship is the reason.

Do not just purchase a device labeled "Ergonomic" because of its advertising. Use guiding biomechanical principles and knowledge of causal relationships to steer the buying.

Know This: It is not about GADGETS, it is about the application, PROPER application!

Research and analysis will determine pain causation and steps to take. Trial and refinement will help lead to practical solutions. The BYTR FYTR Manual (Part III) contains sources, examples, and applications.

How to combat the lies.

Understand that computers and peripherals are now a significant integral part of our lives. Snapchat, Facebook, Twitter, Pinterest, Reddit, Instagram, games, streaming videos, and smartphones are also time sinks as a cultural phenomenon.

Perhaps enlist an individual knowledgeable about computer injuries and learned in the ways of prevention and solutions to determine effective purchases. In finding such an individual, perform your due diligence ensuring they are of professional level. If they cannot adequately and easily describe how they will reduce your pain, they are amateur con-artists, offering token instantiated talk of poorly planned pseudo-solutions and will undoubtedly cost you time, effort and money.

Technology is seriously addicting or required and will always have some Human interface. Hence any continued repetitive actions or postures will always be invitations for biting. Hands, feet, wrists, neck, eyes, back, or legs; all are vulnerable. There will always be opportunity for false truths regarding devices to take hold. These camouflaged BYTRs are everywhere, relentless, and unforgiving. They don't care.

Beware of them and those who purport to help you but in actuality do not or cannot.

Watch out for them, both of them!

Beware of two Voodoo Ergonomics variations

These often do more harm than good,

Fake Practitioners
So-called professionals touting themselves Ergonomic specialists abound with limited knowledge bases and less than effective skillsets. Only interested in selling a product or providing superficial ineffective analyses, they offer no real deliverable. Their heart may be in the right place, but they fall short because of inadequate training, expertise, experience, or caring. Watch out for those with only a weekend certification. Ensure they truly have your wellness as a priority

Fake Devices.
Many devices (computer or otherwise) touted and advertised as "Ergonomic," have no substantial effort, data or design to support their claim. It is merely fluff. Placing this word in their advertising copy attempts to lure a purchase with fake promises. Investigation and evaluation are the most important actions before your investment.

Remember, there is no such thing as an ergonomic anything. Using the best ergonomic device in the world wrong could make you worse.

Meanwhile: Peruse these examples using the term Ergonomic as FAKE NEWS making these devices themselves contributor to injury!

A definitive BYTR Pain inducing device for wrists, hands, and forearms *(see p.259, 261, & 266)*

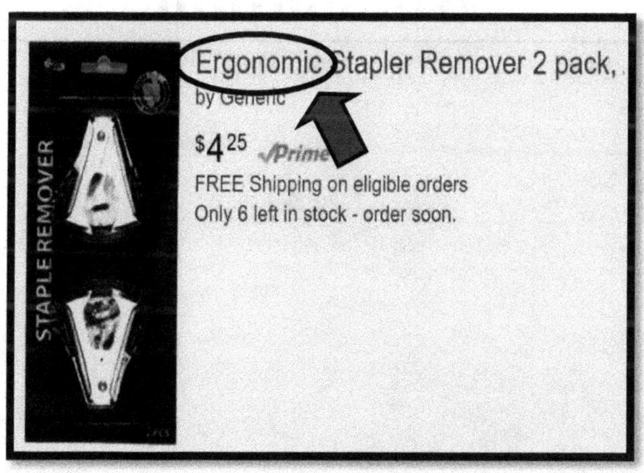

"Ergonomic" Staple Remover
A known BYTR pain inducing device
(see p.259, 261, & 266)

Find real solutions in BYTR FYTR Field Manual.

Section II

Addendum

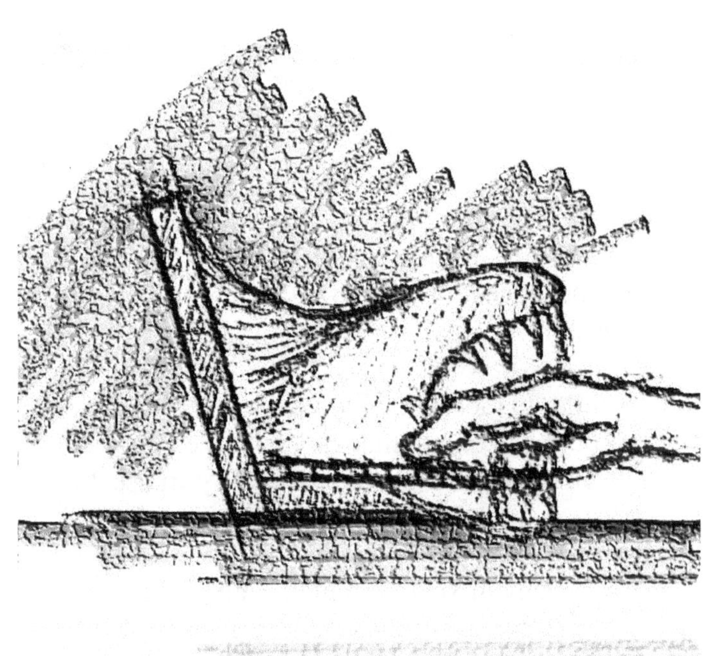

BYTR Attacks the Author!

A True Story

BYTR Attacks the Author

I, too, am a victim of BYTR, believe it or not.

By now, I know these creatures deeply; we battle frequently. Sometimes they win, sometimes I win. Mostly I win.

In crafting this book, I have sat, stood and perched at my computer or laptop, at coffee shops, libraries, or the kitchen table, detailing BYTR aggressions, who and what they are, finding and designing the personae of these tormentors.

Similar to most computer users, I keep working through the minor attacks. I have a calling, a high inspiration to deliver a message, a purpose, helping users *out* of pain. This is what I do.

Like many of you, I am held captive at my computer being engrossed with a sense of self-satisfaction and having a great deal of fun.

These predators have now become friends, enemies, compatriots, and subjects of fascination. BYTR is now a significant element in my life. Immersed while documenting their evil machinations, hours vanish blissfully.

I look at the clock because my fingers are numb, my back is in agony and my derrière is screaming. Otherwise, I would continue, oblivious to everything, BYTR included.

Time for a break? No, no-just keep going, an irresistible allurement, BYTR calls and there is writing, work, and research awaiting. Ignore the pain as adventures present themselves to explore and document. I cannot stop!

Sound familiar? Yes, ignoring hunger and sleep, I am captured just like Skinner's rats (p. 34).

And yet, as some might imagine I have the best custom designed high-tech Ergonomic workstation in the world. The key is: it's crafted specific for me***, just as yours should be crafted specific to you. Otherwise, it is not Ergonomic!***

My workstation continually changes, depending on my mood, my tasking needs, or my body requirements at any specific time. It changes as I change. I try new things applicable to my tasks and the way I work. I keep some; I dismiss some. Changes occur daily, some are kept for the long-term. Some are custom fabricated in our Ergonomics Lab. The point is to keep exploring looking for the optimum solution.

Avoiding BYTR is like a game of dodgeball. I must pay strict attention to my adversary and keep moving in order not to get hit. Constant anticipation of The Collective is a must. We all must follow the Master's teachings (p.149) to appreciate this basic form of warfare and gamesmanship. It comes down to ***us*** versus ***The Collective.***

I well know these BYTRS because I am targeted and continually assaulted by their destructive actions. Fortunately, I have weapons, resources and a lifetime of knowledge to fight back. But still I cannot avoid them. Like dodgeball, every player, no matter how skilled, eventually gets hit.

Constant vigilance is paramount. Inattention results in severe numbness, tingling, or pain, like many of the injured workers I am chartered to help, perhaps even yourself.

Thankfully, my profession does not manacle me to my desk like many of the injured workers I see, except such times when entrapped while documenting BYTR exploits. I have the freedom to leave the ball and chain workstation scenario and can journey out for a change of positioning and activities. And yet I still succumb, returning to the BYTR allurement that again captures me as it captures you, placing me back in peril.

And when I succumb, like you, BYTR pain comes from intense and lengthy computer tasking. However, my pain can be short-lived if I make appropriate adjustments to my workstation. Sometimes I enlist a BYTR FYTR colleague, for an objective opinion. A fresh set of credentialed and experienced eyes is always helpful. Being uncommon, they are sometimes hard to find.

Of course, you could become one or get one.

How I Fight the BYTRs

Thankfully, I know how to recover by getting away from my technological devices.

I know by unplugging myself from the grid with a beach vacation or a spa day, my ailments will diminish or even disappear. The same results are attainable for everyone.

This is the first clue to BYTR fighting. Meanwhile- even with mini or maxi breaks, at work or play, BYTRS are still there, attacking at any opportunity.

As a practiced FYTR, I have learned to:

- Change my equipment
- Take my breaks
- Look out the window
- Alter my habits
- Alter my methods
- Change my chair
- Move my monitor
- Change out or move my keyboard
- Get new (designated computer) glasses
- Change character size on my monitor
- Change the way I sit
- Change the way I type/keyboard/swipe
- Change the way I mouse
- Change my mouse

- Get a massage occasionally–hot tubs for muscle relaxation are also excellent (however, you only feel great until returning to pain inducing workstations, work tasks, or work tools)

All this should be second nature to one having aspirations to becoming an effective BYTR FYTR.

Sometimes simple ongoing changes with complete awareness and preparedness will bring your discomfort level down low enough that your body stamina can withstand other physical onslaughts.

I know I can stave off BYTR attacks and continue the marathon keyboard sessions, and you can do the same.

Weapons of self-defense are presented in Section III. Use and apply them well.

Give a call if you need more combat instruction.

I would love to hear how you battled them and how you won. If you haven't won, I would be pleased to offer sage advice (Professional Courtesy).

Consider it my gift to you.

I can be found at:
www.ergoinc.com
(just mention this book)

BYTR Buzzwords

(Glossary)

Layman Definitions
Of
Commonly Known
Computer Induced Injuries
&
Lexicon

For Everyone to Understand

Most Commonly Known Computer Induced Injuries

Carpal Tunnel Syndrome (aka CTS)

Pain or throbbing in the wrist area, mostly on the bottom, often encircling the wrist–symptoms include numbness and tingling, affecting the palm, thumb, index, middle, half the ring fingers, but not the pinky (enervated by the ulnar nerve AKA "funny bone" nerve– sometimes CTS pain moves up forearms.

Eye Strain

Eyes also have muscles–six tiny ones which spin your eyeball in its socket, and a ring of super tiny ones around the lens adjusting its thickness for focus, the same muscle type you have in the rest of your body only much smaller–these also fatigue and become painful (or strained) from overuse, or static eye (ball) positioning, resulting in typical muscle strain type pain.

Lateral Epicondylitis-AKA Tennis Elbow

Point pain at the outside "bump" of either elbow having several causes-mostly the extensor musculature attaching to the upper arm bone at the yes, lateral epicondyle–origins are varied, with many related to keyboard, mouse or chair (armrest impact).

Muscle Strain

Pain flares from a dull ache to severe pain in the strained (overused/overtaxed) muscle area when pushed past its strength or functional limits impacting the movement of body area serviced by that specific muscle.

Most Commonly Known Computer Induced Injuries–con't

Numbness

Loss of feeling commonly in the hands & fingers because of nerve compression upstream at the armpit (thoracic outlet syndrome), at the wrist (carpal tunnel syndrome), the neck (muscle tightness / cervical impingement) or elbow (cubital tunnel entrapment) areas. Leg numbness is caused by nerve compression in the low back or buttocks area.

Sciatica

Pain along the sciatic nerve track running from the low back through the buttock area, down the back of both legs–often through the entire leg to the heels–also affects adjacent muscles–tingling and numbness are oftentimes present.

Tendinitis

Inflammation of various tendons connecting muscles to bones, anywhere in the body–flares as mild to severe pain in the tendon sheaths of whatever specific tendon(s) is being activated or overused.

Tingling

A sensation of ants crawling over the skin, also known as sparks, caused by blood constriction affecting hands, fingers, toe, and feet–also caused by nerve compression upstream.

Lesser Known Computer Induced Injuries

Bulging Disc–AKA Herniated Disc

Your discs are like jelly doughnuts having a squishy middle. When you bite a jelly doughnut, the jelly often squishes out onto your shirt. Similarly, pressure on the discs squeezes the squishy middle out toward the back or posterior area. This jelly now places pressure on a neural track and *voilà*; you have pain in the muscles enervated by the compressed neural tracks. Mild to severe pain flares down the sciatic nerve running down the back of the leg, also triggering pain in leg muscles. Pain also tracks around the hip to the front of the pelvis or leg areas. You want to do everything possible to avoid or lessen the pain from a bulging disc, like get a good chair or standing workstation.

Cubital Tunnel Entrapment / Syndrome

Mild to severe pain or ache in the elbow underside from repetitive motion or from contact (impact trauma) with chair armrests–also, leaning on elbows on desktops can cause impact trauma to underside of elbow from the desktop edge; all from compression of the ulnar nerve (funny bone) as it passes through the tunnel in the elbow. This compression is sometimes thought to be caused by continually keeping the elbow bent during computer tasks.

Lesser Known
Computer Induced Injuries–con't

Femoral Triangle Compression

The small inner frontal area connecting the leg to the torso, called the femoral triangle contains a group of nerves and blood vessels. Sitting in a chair with upper legs 90° to the torso crushes this triangle, decreases blood supply, and squashes neural tracks, similar to standing on a garden hose which restricts water (blood) flow. Without an adequate blood supply, legs develop pain and aches or go to sleep (especially harmful for those with diabetes or other vascular issues).

Gluteal Compression

Sitting all day crushes the derriere, flattening and compressing blood vessels and sciatic nerves causing numbness, itching, and ache.

Impact Trauma

Your pain reaction to body parts repeatedly or continually contacting a solid object causing you to move or hold that body part away from the offending object. Sometimes It causes an actual diagnosable injury. Also known to cause static loading on another body part, it can place significant stressors on yet another, such as compressing nerves or vasculature.

Examples: Banging your elbows, either inside or outside of high chair arms forcing arm abduction or adduction affecting shoulders, also causing neural compression.

Lesser Known Computer Induced Injuries–con't

Impact Trauma–con't

Examples–con't:

Continually resting wrists or heel of the hand on desk edge or on keyboard edge results in holding or hovering hands constantly (static loading) over a keyboard.

Medial Epicondylitis- AKA Golfer's Elbow

Point pain at the inside "bump" of either elbow having several causes, with many related to bad postures using the keyboard or mouse.

Neural Compression–AKA pinched nerve

Squeezing or squashing nerve tracks, from sitting on your derrière (crushing sciatic nerve) to tight muscles clamping down on inner or adjacent nerve tracks. Also caused by innocuous things such as overly tight watchbands, stiff belts, highly form-fitting shirts, pants, or shoes.

Static Loading or Positioning

The constant or continuous non-moving positioning of arms, legs, backs, shoulders, etc. places a significant and continual strain on muscles. Like isometric exercise, it appears no effort is being expended. The army formation of "parade rest" is actually more difficult than standing at attention, because of the static loading on musculature. Leaning forward in the chair all day is an example of static loading on the back and neck musculature causing pain.

Lesser Known Ergonomics Lexicon

Charlatan Certificants

A term likened to those having a minor level certificate (4-hour online course rewarded with a "certificate" suitable for framing) who boast of skills and experience as a "Certified Ergonomist," having no real interest in advancing their proficiency or knowledge, often doing more harm than good.

Ergometrics

This word does not exist in the Merriam-Webster Dictionary, the Oxford Dictionary, or Wikipedia. It is often confused with biometrics and frequently misused by those who are attempting to show some a semblance of knowledge–not to be confused with an Ergometer which is an exercise machine.

Voodoo Ergonomics

A term coined by professional ergonomists relating to products marketed as ergonomic attempting to sway the lay customer into a purchase whereas the product has no real basis or design towards ergonomic truths–overall a sleazy marketing ploy to capture those unaware–definitely a *caveat emptor.*

Also relates to professionals who perform shoddy work at cut-rate, sometimes inflated fees with a useless or ineffective work product leaving injured workers in pain with no real solution.

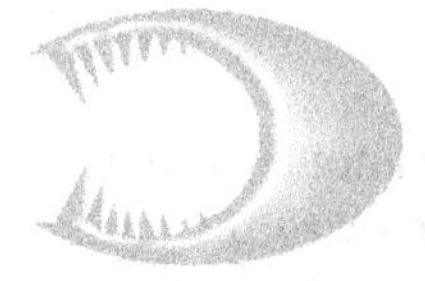

Beware The BYTR!

The BYTR Challenge

THE BYTR CHALLENGE

My Dear Human, here I present a challenge to you-a contest, a game, a sport to see who can emerge victoriously. The gauntlet is thrown.

Your interaction with The Collective can be likened to a game of chess, based on adversarial interaction and moves in turn. Defeating the opponent is the intent and goal. Your body, psyche, and livelihood are the prizes.

Win them if you can…

Your move…
My move…

Can you block my knight?
Can I take your queen?

Can you anticipate my attack?
Can I take a bite from you?

Who has the checkmate?

You? Or The BYTR?

Can you succeed or easily falter and forfeit?

The stakes are high!

BYTRs have little to lose

You have your health and livelihood to lose.

Are you prepared to play?

The Challenge
Are you ready to play, Human?

Will You Defeat Me?

You Have Much to Lose!

You have been warned.

And now, you must beware!

Beware, be *very* aware.

Because now, now.

BYTR is COMING FOR YOU–it is simply a matter of time.

Bite…Bite…***Byte.***

CAN YOU WIN BACK YOUR HEALTH, CAREER, AND MEANS TO SUPPORT YOUR FAMILY?

We shall see.

Prepare yourself to play.

Ready your game face Human.

Proceed if you dare!

You Are
Now Ready to
Undertake this
Challenge,

Ready to
Become a Real…

To help you on your mission, The BYTR FYTR BRIGADE presents your first weapon, this copy of THE BYTR FYTR Field Manual. Guard it well; use it to engage the BYTRS and to win the battle against your pain.

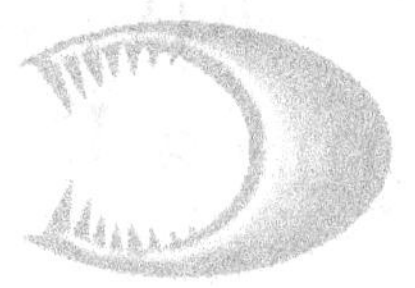

Beware The BYTR!

SECTION III

THE BYTR FYTR FIELD MANUAL

Ways and means to engage and defeat your adversary

Official Stationary of

THE BYTR FYTR BRIGADE

Publishers of the BYTR FYTR Manual

To: New BYTR FYTR recruits
Subject: Welcoming Letter
Date: Today

Welcome to the BYTR FYTR Brigade!

I have accepted the responsibility of providing you with this official BYTR FYTR Manual. It contains instructions and means known as effective against personal BYTR attacks.

IMPORTANT: All such weapons have a unique and proper application for specific injuries and pain patterns. First, determine the injury/pain cause. Second, apply the appropriate weapon (FYTR / Friendly Device), then observe and analyze for success. Third, if ineffective, reassess and correct by installing a new application. ***Repeat as necessary, until pain is diminished,*** injury addressed, and the attack lessened.

I will be at your side as long as you wish, offering guidance and helping you meet the challenge until it can indeed be said you have joined the ranks of the FYTR Brigade.

Remember, defeat only comes the moment pain returns, and you quit FYTING. Follow these teachings well.

Best of Luck FYTR.

I Remain,

Your Mentor

AKA The Frequent FYTR

Your health, career & personal life are our highest concerns.

THE BYTR FYTR FIELD MANUAL

WEAPONS & METHODS TO COMBAT INJURY AND PAIN CAUSED BY THE BYTRS

PREPARED BY

The BYTR FYTR BRIGADE

Authors Declaration

NO product is universally "Ergonomic", and it is best to have a TRAINED, EXPERIENCED, OR CREDENTIALED professional to select the best products for specific situations and application.

Otherwise, you are merely shooting in the dark and will likely miss your target.

Some would think because specific products are included in this book, I am endorsing them and may even be on the manufacturers' payroll. Let it be known these mentions are ***NOT*** product promotions in any way!

I am illustrating their benefits and show successes and even critiques. The point is to demonstrate how these devices can be used to the advantage of businesses and mostly for the reduction of your pain.

Although not endorsing them, I am pleased in presenting their positive elements and state the reasons. Some work wonderfully well (and this is key) in **the right application.**

Remember, there is no such thing as an Ergonomic anything. I could give you the best Ergonomic device in the world, and if you use it wrong, *you could get worse.*

BYTR FYTR–(bī′tər fī′tər) *n.*
Pronunciation: *Biter Fighter*

A relatively unknown term used to identify individuals having the courage to battle against predators known as BYTRs.

Known to use various weapons, methods and knowledge to heal or prevent misery from BYTR (computer) induced pain and injury.

BYTR–(bī′tər) n.
Pronunciation: *Biter*

An ethereal predator known to attack from all computer devices (as identified in this manual).

A derivative of BYTE, a data-storage capacity of eight bits, the smallest unit of addressable computer memory.

BYTR Device–(bī′tər di vis′) *n.*
Pronunciation: *Biter Device*

A BYTR FYTR Brigade designation of any professional or personal device having a causal relationship to pain, connected to a computer or not. Many stand-alone computer devices may never trigger pain or discomfort for some users. The name BYTR DEVICE can be assigned to any device, tool, or equipment piece that causes pain by its usage-repetitive or not. Not every computer device will turn into a BYTR Device, but every device might become one.

FYTR Device–(fī′tər di vis′) *n.*

Pronunciation: *Fighter Device*

A device used by BYTR FYTRs to replace any specific BYTR DEVICE known to cause specific user pain and injury.

Replacement often occurs after a FYTR analysis has determined a casual effect of symptomology from any BYTR DEVICE. FYTRs include users who are taking a proactive approach in their healthcare.

Friendly Device–(frend′lē di vis′) *n.*

Pronunciation: *Friendly Device*

These have little or minimal impact on user anatomy and can be used for indefinite periods without any symptomology.

Any Friendly Device can easily and *instantly* become a BYTR Device, providing little or no warning. Lack of any follow-up corrective user action under duress will escalate the BYTR syndrome.

Knowledge or FYTR training is essential to determine if any device has a hazardous potential or if precautions can keep any device a Friendly Device.

"The general who wins

the battle

makes many calculations

in his temple

before the battle is fought."

Sun Tzu–*The Art of War*
500 B.C.

Instructions for:
PLANNING your attack on The BYTR

Follow this methodology for yourself or someone else as the basics for defense.

1. Perform a detailed biomechanical and pain trigger observation and analysis*
2. Correlate pain to postures, position or improperly applied device
3. Determine an appropriate solution by serious research for the device, position or method
4. Apply corrective measures or devices
5. Follow-up and determine the effectiveness
6. Modify the solution as necessary
7. Follow-up again to ensure the solution(s) are fully effective

Weapons Cache & Supply Depots

It is essential to know where to find the weapons, tools, and equipment needed for your BYTR battles. These weapons suppliers will help any FYTR requesting assistance. Contact them when your plan of attack is underway and you seek to turn any BYTR Device to a real FYTR Device (*as determined by factual analysis*).

ERGOGUYS

ERGOGUYS is in sunny Arizona, with a lot of days above 100 degrees and not much rain. This isn't necessarily a bad thing as we spend all our time working in the dark in front of computer screens researching new and exciting products to offer our customers.

We're always looking for the "next best thing" so if you have seen a product you really like that we don't carry, drop us an email with the pertinent information and we'll be happy to look into it.

Unlike some retailers, we aren't ashamed to say we are in business to make a profit. After all, we have families to support. But we have low overhead and can pass on the savings to our customers. We figure that if we treat you right, you'll keep coming back and maybe even tell your friends or co-workers about us. www.ergoguys.com 602-354-4190

Sources

Weapons Cache & Supply Depots

ERGOBUYER

Ergobuyer® began in 1997 as an advertising based buyer's guide to the ergonomics marketplace, which was housed within the ergoweb.com site. ***We quickly found that some marketers were making unsubstantiated or grandiose claims about the ergonomics of their products***. So in 2006 we embarked on a campaign to raise the credibility of ergonomic claims, reformulating the Ergobuyer brand into a separate company, and then into an online store:

"No gimmicks. No fads. Only effective, reliable, ergonomically designed products, satisfaction guaranteed."

Ergobuyer has since served businesses and consumers with trusted, reliable products, from a trusted, reliable source. We as ergonomists, use and evaluate the products personally invoking a "litmus" test before placing them on our web.

www.ergobuyer.com
866-515-1323 or 435-214-4269
36600 N. Pima Road, Suite 303-9
Carefree, AZ 85377 USA

P.S. Quit laughing, this is our real address! Carefree is a real city, just north of Scottsdale, and it's a perfect place for an ergonomics company. We can't guarantee a 'carefree' life, but our products, services and customer service ethic can move you in that direction.

Table of Contents

Table of Contents–con't

Table of Contents–con't

ADDENDUM to BYTR FYTR Field Manual

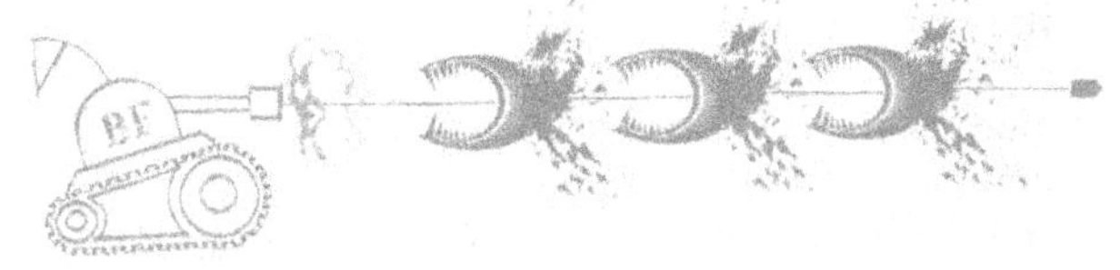
BF

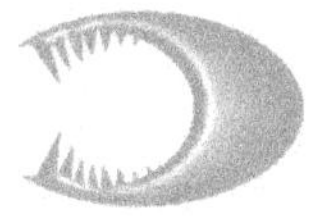

BYTR Devices & YOUR DEFENSE WEAPONS

OVERVIEW

BYTR DEVICES

WARNING:

DANGEROUS
AND
HIGHLY PAIN INDUCING

FYTR Rating Scale

Pain Generation Potential: **High**
Fytr Rating Scale: **High**
Recovery Index: **Medium to High**

INTRODUCTION & OVERVIEW

The following identifies computer input and workstation equipment as BYTR Devices continually used by BYTR entities for pain development. Excessive physical contact with these devices prolongs pain and injuries.

Each BYTR DEVICE analysis details methods for reducing its damaging qualities, AKA FYTR Device application.

Understand the BYTR Devices contained within are not inclusive and that your adversaries have many more, some are unknown, some not yet developed or deployed.

Your FYTR Weaponry is the same. Those illustrated are not the total available to you. Likewise, there are many more, some unknown to you, some not yet developed or deployed.

You must use your skills of observation and knowledge in determining how the enemy uses their arsenal to formulate countermeasures. Choose wisely for proper and practical applications.

Remember your training. Repeat observations, applications, and evaluations until pain reduction below threshold occurs.

Use this information well; it may well save your health, career, or livelihood.

WELL-KNOWN HAZARDOUS BYTR DEVICES

CAUSING YOUR PAIN & INJURY

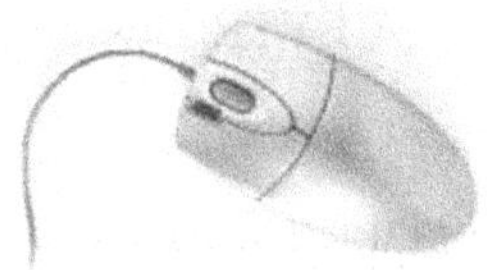

BYTR Device #1
The Mouse

BYTR Device #2
The Keyboard

BYTR Device #3
Computer Task Chair

BYTR Device #4
The Monitor,
Lines-of-sight
Distance-of-focus

Beware of these common computer devices. These and others have the potential to allow the BYTRs full access to any user anatomy.

LESSER-KNOWN HAZARDOUS BYTR DEVICES

CAUSING YOUR PAIN & INJURY

BYTR Device #5
The Footrest

BYTR Device #6
High Desktop

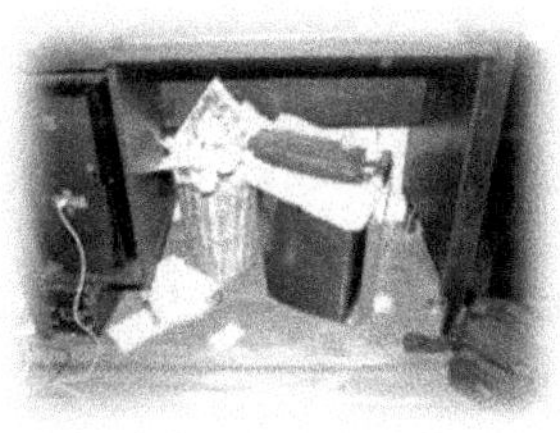

BYTR Device #7
The Wastebasket

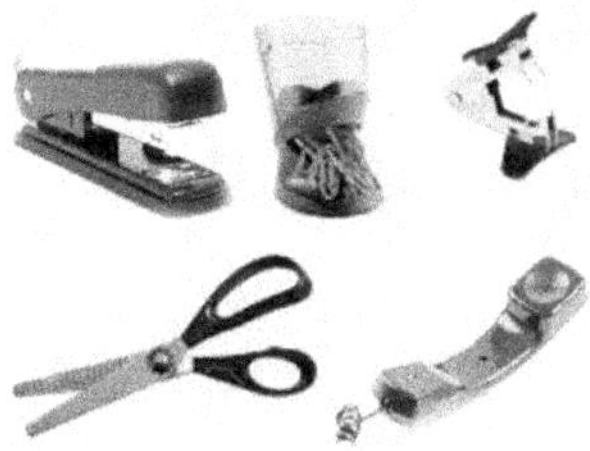

BYTR Device #8
Office Tools

Know and familiarize yourself thoroughly with these. Detailed understanding allows you to apply effective defenses against all BYTR DEVICES.

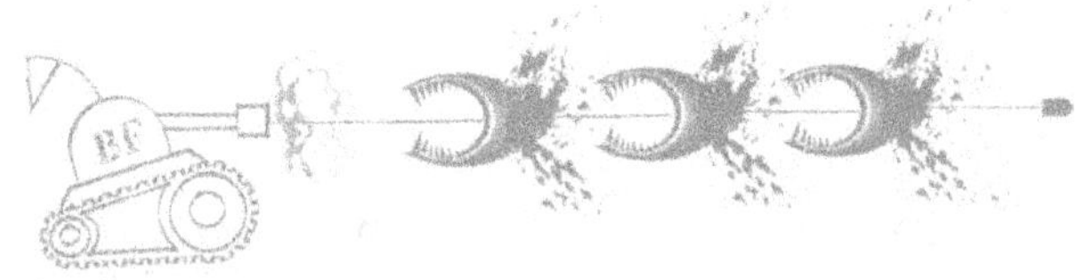

MOUSE
PAIN GENERATION

BYTR PAIN
DEVICE #1

SECTION A

Kensington
Logitech

User Danger Level Rating

BYTR Pain Generation Potential: **High**
FYTR Alert Level: **High**
Recovery Potential Index: **Medium to High**

THE BYTR MOUSE

SECTION A

The computer mouse is well known as a device for imparting high-level RMI, carpal tunnel syndrome, tendinitis and other pain in the mousing hand and arm. Hazard comes with long usage and adverse positioning also affecting backs, arms, and shoulders.

A vast majority of computer users continually handle a mouse or a touchpad through an entire workday, including engineers, graphic designers, 3D illustrators, accountants, etc.

The pain and injury stem from continual hand contact in moving, clicking and scrolling. More contact results in more opportunity for The BYTRs, especially true with exaggerated hand/finger/wrist positioning and movement. The mouse is a natural pathway for The BYTR Collective to cause harm.

Using a mouse (any shape, form or brand) on a high desktop (unlike on an underdesk keyboard tray) has significant potential for injury and pain.

If pain is present in fingers, hand, wrist or forearm, the mouse should be the first device analyzed.

BYTR MOUSE OVERVIEW

SECTION A.1

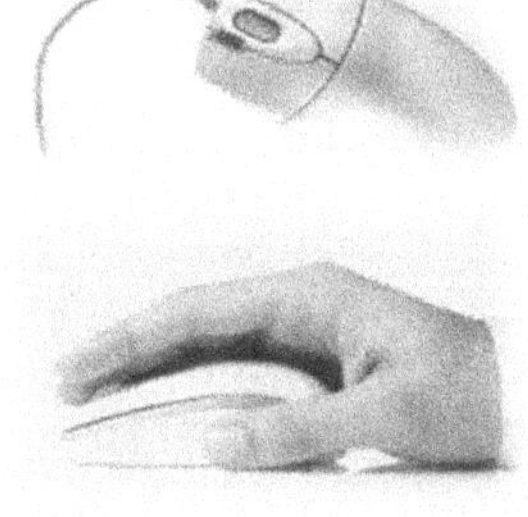

Typical mouse–high pain generation potential

Subtle continual muscle activation, positioning (static loading) and significant repetitive motions (dynamic loading) in handling are high-level pain triggers

A tight continuous grip using thumb and small finger, continuous scroll using index finger are all triggers for hand, finger and forearm pain

Clues to determine pain generation:

- Tense or tight finger positioning (see photo above)
- Maintaining a tight grip when the hand is merely resting on the mouse
- Movement of mouse left and right, "hinged" at the wrist as in waving "hello"
- Movement of mouse front to rear, "hinged" at the wrist as in waving "goodbye" without moving the forearm

BYTR MOUSE FYTR FACTS

SECTION A.2

- ***The mouse is the most common pain trigger in computer workstations***
- Supplied to the user population by default-not every user will have pain generation from the mouse
- A high rate of recovery and symptomology reduction results with the replacement of BYTR Devices with friendly FYTR Devices
- Changing to a different mouse (shape) daily or weekly reduces hand musculature RMI with different hand postures or positioning–color also alters mood affecting manipulation posture
- Some perceive it as a real mouse, with an unconscious severe tight grip to "prevent it from running away"
- Switching to a left-handed mouse use as a remedy for right-hand symptomology is ineffective–moving the mouse to the other hand often results with identical symptomology due to positioning, the method of use or body type, all dependent upon user susceptibility
- Highly recommended for laptop use eliminating hazardous touchpad usage
- Some form of mouse is destined to be an input device for the foreseeable future

Outward rotation from body midline, arm and hand contacting the desktop, extended reach, arm abduction and forearm impact on a high desktop are at-risk conditions–

don't do this

Outward arm rotation with arm abduction and wrists contacting high desktop are pain triggers–

don't do this

BYTR MOUSE PAIN SPECIFICS

INJURIES & SYMPTOMOLOGIES

SECTION A.3

A.3.1 Primary Targets of High-Level Pain & Injury

- Wrists–carpal tunnel syndrome/tendinitis
- Index & middle Fingers–numbness, tingling
- Small fingers–ache, cramping
- Thumbs–joint inflammation deterioration
- Hands–tendinitis, cramping

A.3.2 Secondary Targets due to Mouse Positioning

- Forearm–muscle strain/tendinitis/cramping
- Elbow–lateral epicondylitis/ulnar nerve entrapment
- Shoulder–bicipital groove inflammation & rotator cuff musculature overloading

A.3.3 Destructive Capability Potential

- High trigger levels
- High to low- level pain–nagging & annoying increasing to highly distracting or disabling
- Forced time off work
- Limits use of hand and fingers in other tasks
- Causes the inability to perform personal tasks

A.3.4 Symptomology

- Severe pain/constant ache
- Numbness
- Tingling (sparks)
- Articulation sensory loss
- Inability to move hands and wrists

A.3.5 Potential Symptomology levels

- Constant to severe (debilitating)

BYTR MOUSE PAIN DEVELOPMENT

BODY AREAS & CAUSES

SECTION A.4

Primary Body Areas Affected & Causes

A.4.1 Wrist

- Wrist movement–Left & right swing (waving hello) causing repetitive motions
- Wrist movement–Forward and backward motion causing repetitive motions
- Poor hand/mouse positioning causing (palmar side) pressure contact of wrist bones against desk surface

A.4.2 Fingers

- Repeated index, middle, ring finger clicking–especially with high force grip on the mouse
- Continual scrolling wheel using the index or middle fingers in “claw’ position and overall high downward force on mouse back using the index or middle finger

A.4.3 Hands

- Too tight grip between thumb and small fingers when clicking, moving and holding the mouse
- High downward pressure on top of the mouse during movement
- Overuse of the side thumb button click

BYTR MOUSE PAIN DEVELOPMENT

BODY AREAS & CASES–CON'T

SECTION A.5

Secondary Body Areas Affected & Causes

A.5.1 Forearm

- Finger forward and backward motion (pulling mouse forward & backward) continually activates forearm musculature causing fatigue, cramping, and inflammation
- Holding hand in outward rotation from body
- Wrist movement–Left & right swing repetitive motions causing musculature overuse
- Wrist movement–Forward and rearward repetitive motions causing musculature overuse with resulting cramping or ache

A.5.2 Elbow

- Hand/arm held in outward rotation from torso–static loading with muscle strain

A.5.3 Shoulder

- Hand/arm held in outward rotation from the torso–static loading with muscle strain
- Hand/arm held away from the body with a high elbow using the mouse on a desktop instead of in a lower position

MOUSE FYTR WEAPONS

SELECTED WEAPONS TO FIGHT & CONQUER THE BYTR MOUSE

KNOWN TO BE HIGHLY EFFECTIVE FOR REDUCING PAIN & INJURY

Kensington Trackball
Contour RollerMouse

FYTR Rating Scale

Pain Reduction from Mouse Use: **High**
Fytr Rating Scale: **High**
Recovery Index: **High**

THE TRACKBALL

APPLICATIONS OVERVIEW

SECTION AA

The Trackball is effective in offloading tight grips and tight musculature allowing a more relaxed hand and associated forearm posture. However, if improperly placed on high desktops, it can continue causing forearm (and shoulder) problems

Location and style of click buttons and scrolling mechanism is critical. Inappropriate applications (button design or location) have a potential to (inadvertently) continue pain trigger. Previously unknown issues or symptomology may appear and if so, follow up with further analysis determining if a more appropriate trackball or input device is necessary.

Some users adapt immediately–some have a significant learning curve. Thus for addressing the original pain triggers, complete awareness and functional usage training is required.

Trackballs are available in different sizes, configurations and applications. Spin-off high-tech joysticks are also available to address discomfort.

.

THE KENSINGTON TRACKBALL(S)

SECTION AA.1

Expert Mouse

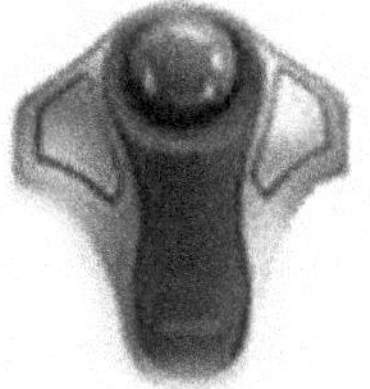

Orbit

www.kensington.com

Slimblade

Awareness Factor:

- Each has specific characteristics (style, shape, ball size & location, button number & placement) requiring consideration
- Different hand size, type and location of pain, type of injury, and temperament are deciding factors for application
- An application must be specific to the injury or symptomology
- The wrong application means an unsuccessful solution

FYTR FACTS

HOW THE KENSINGTON TRACKBALL(S) REDUCES PAIN

SECTION AA.1.1

- Programmable buttons allow changing of the clicking postures eliminating single keyboard repetitive motions–such as pressing <esc>, <tab>, <backspace>, and <enter> keys with adverse wrist postures (ulnar deviation)
- Encourages hands, wrist, and finger into *body-neutral* position by offloading significant muscle activity such as gripping postures
- Allows full use of the hand, wrist, and finger action with less effort using a more relaxed posture
- Uses a more natural posture and position of the hand and wrist in performing the cursor move movement
- Useful for left and right-hands
- Installed in parallel to a mouse allows using both devices enabling users a long duration to become accustomed to the new method of cursor movement still keeping the familiar during the adaption period

FYTR FACTS

CHALLENGES & CONSIDERATIONS FOR KENSINGTON APPLICATIONS

SECTION AA.1.2

- Can be misapplied to address forearm pain when the entire hand (and arm) still remains on a high desktop
- Balls come in different sizes: small, medium, or large–the ball must be appropriate for the user's hand size and finger length/mobility/function
- Overall the trackball device style must be appropriate for specifically identified pain triggers
- Users often improperly use fingertips attempting to "roll" or "grip" the ball
- Users often press down hard on ball still causing pressure to the palm
- Poor arm positioning can also result in pressure on the palm or underside of the wrist
- Some users will have difficulty adapting and keeping their mouse installed in parallel (allowing both to function simultaneously) will make the adaption period less stressful

THE CONTOUR ROLLERMOUSE

APPLICATIONS OVERVIEW

SECTION AA.2

- Effective in offloading all tight grips and musculature posture (static loading) by a more relaxed hand positioning
- Eliminates tight grip and hand swings (outward rotation & extended reach).
- Allows a more gentle motion with less muscular activation (less hand, finger & forearm muscular activity (static loading)
- Some users adapt readily, others require gentle coaxing
- Reduces significant pain, numbness, and tingling (when used correctly) and is also more productive as users spend less time searching for the mouse
- Large palm rests (if properly adjusted) will help with forearm support
- A detailed setup specific to the user and workstation will have the most potent defense against adverse hand, wrist and arm postures.
- Perfectly adaptable to coexist with an external mouse or trackball for fine (graphics) control

CONTOUR ROLLERMOUSE

SECTION AA.2.1

Contour RollerMouse

Contour RollerMouse
www.contourdesign.com

Awareness Factor:

- Unique configuration eliminates the traditional handheld mouse
- Minimizes significant pain associated with typical mouse usage
- Keeps both hands in the keyboard center minimizing any external rotation
- Removes any extended reach normally used to reach a mouse or other input device at the keyboard side
- Adaptability is the primary user hurdle
- Wrist/palm support conversions allow custom adaptability for specific applications of hand or wrist positioning

FYTR FACTS

HOW THE CONTOUR ROLLERMOUSE REDUCES PAIN

SECTION AA.2.3

- Applicable for both hands
- Eliminates any outward rotation of the forearm/elbow to reach mouse located to either side of the keyboard
- Eliminates the concept of using the mouse on the non-dominant hand to give the dominant hand a rest which usually results in the non-dominant hand becoming inflamed
- Eliminates any extended reach affecting forearm/shoulder musculature
- Programmable buttons such as the commonly used cut and paste eliminate double key keyboard usage by keeping hands centered and in a more relaxed posture
- RollerMouse eliminates any hand grip or position triggering pain
- RollerMouse moves cursor using fingers, palm, or thumb all independently
- Provides a beneficial elevated or angled, palm rest (not wrist rest)

FYTR FACTS

CHALLENGES & CONSIDERATIONS FOR THE CONTOUR ROLLERMOUSE

SECTION AA.2.4

- User initial reaction is often one of surprise
- Aversion to change is an occasional challenge
- Potential improper application for users having finger flexion or movement pain generation
- Potential improper application for users having with inward arm rotation pain generation–i.e. shoulder issues
- If not set up correctly relative to the keyboard angle, proximity, or overall orientation)

FYTR FACTS

SUPPLEMENTAL

SECTION AA.2.5

- Every FYTR must know RollerMouse principles to ensure a thorough understanding of applications and of where and when to implement.
- Very applicable to solving significant pain issues

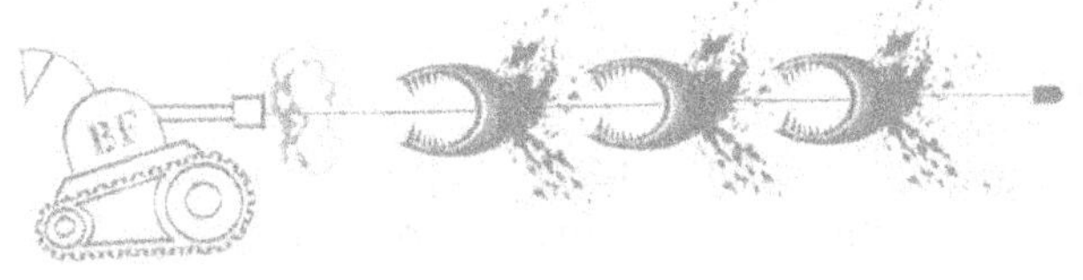

KEYBOARD PAIN GENERATION

BYTR PAIN DEVICE #2

SECTION B

User Danger Level Rating

BYTR Pain Generation Potential: **High**
FYTR Alert Level: **High**
Recovery Potential Index: **Medium to High**

THE BYTR KEYBOARD

SECTION B

Keyboards are the primary physical connection between users and computers. Well-known intense usage triggers high-level RMI, carpal tunnel syndrome, tendinitis and other debilitating pain in hands, wrists, and arms.

A vast majority of computer users, including accountants, legal and administrative assistants, writers, etc. perform a continuous large number of keystrokes throughout any workday.

Pain and injury stem from highly repetitive finger motions with minimal movement (static loading/posturing) of hands & arms, constantly tensing associated musculature.

With more keyboard finger contact, the more opportunity for the BYTRs, resulting in increasing risk for pain and crippling injury.

Using a typical keyboard on a high desktop also imparts additional stressors on elbows, shoulders, upper arms, including necks, and backs, contributing to an increase of potential injury and pain in body areas not associated with keyboard pain.

BYTR KEYBOARD OVERVIEW

SECTION B.1

Typical BYTR keyboard–high pain generator

Strained finger positioning

Subtle static positioning and significant repetitive motions in key strikes are main pain triggers

Adverse finger positioning

Continuous and excessive stressful finger positioning eventually results in pain and injury

BYTR KEYBOARD PAIN SPECIFICS

INJURIES & SYMPTOMOLOGIES

SECTION B.1.1

B.1.1.1 Primary Targets of Pain & Injury

- Wrists
- Fingers
- Hands

B.1.1.2 Secondary Targets of Pain & Injury

- Forearm
- Elbow
- Back/neck

B.1.1.3 Destructive Capability Potential

- High pain trigger levels
- Carpal tunnel syndrome
- Tendinitis
- Tenosynovitis
- Muscle strain/sprain

B.1.1.4 Symptomology

- Pain/Ache
- Numbness
- Tingling (sparks)
- Articulation sensory loss
- Contact stress/point pain AKA impact stress

B.1.1.5 Symptomology levels

- Constant to severe (debilitating)

BYTR KEYBOARD PAIN DEVELOPMENT

BODY AREAS & CAUSES

SECTION B.1.2

Primary Pain Area Specifics

B.1.2.1 Wrist

- Continual wrist movement–Left & right ulnar deviation (wrist turned outward) for orientation to home row
- Extreme ulnar deviation to strike "outboard" keys from home row orientation (using small fingers to hit <enter>, <esc>, <tab>, <bksp> keys)

B.1.2.2 Fingers

- Repeated index finger key striking
- Repeated middle finger key striking
- Repeated thumb space bar striking
- Continual fingers in a "claw" position over the home row in the "at-the-ready" position

B.1.2.3 Hands

- Holding hands in extended (bent up & hovering) position over the home row in the "at-the-ready" position

BYTR KEYBOARD PAIN DEVELOPMENT

BODY AREAS & CAUSES–CON'T

SECTION B.1.3.

Secondary Pain Area Specifics

B.1.3.1 Forearm

- Finger forward and rearward motion continually activates forearm musculature (which moves fingers) causing fatigue and overuse
- Continual hand ulnar deviation or outward rotation also affects forearm musculature

B.1.3.2 Elbow

- Pulling hands to inward rotation often can inadvertently force elbows away from the body

B.1.3.3 Shoulder

- Shoulders keep the upper arms in a static position with elbows pulled away from the torso (abduction) with a resultant tension

B.1.3.4 Neck

- Forced forward lean with bent head to view keyboard stresses neck musculature

B.1.3.5 Upper, Mid & Lower Back

- Forced forward lean (with bent head) to view keyboard stresses back musculature
- Forward lean to engage keyboard pulls torso away from the chair back affecting entire back musculature

KEYBOARD FYTR WEAPONS

SELECTED WEAPONS TO FIGHT & CONQUER THE BYTR KEYBOARD

KNOWN TO BE HIGHLY EFFECTIVE FOR REDUCING PAIN & INJURY

Kinesis Freestyle
Goldtouch
Kinesis Advantage

FYTR Ratings

Pain Reduction from keyboard usage: **High**
Fytr Rating Scale: **High**
Recovery Index: **High**

SELECTED FYTR WEAPONS TO CONQUER THE BYTR KEYBOARD

SECTION BB

The Kinesis Freestyle Keyboard

www.kinesis-ergo.com

Awareness Factor

The Kinesis Freestyle split keyboard enables the moving of hands to a more “outboard” separated position or to a “V” configuration reducing the constant stressors from continually holding hands in a single “tight” together position (as with a typical keyboard). Immediate keyboard movement or placement allows quick hand position changing during marathon keyboarding. The Freestyle “V” configurations have more advantages than the solid one-piece “V” keyboards by having more adjustability in the “V” and angulation when used with a slope kit. Additional benefits are allowing a different independent reach for either forearm.

FYTR FACTS

HOW THE KINESIS FREESTYLE REDUCES PAIN

SECTION BB.1

- Allows placement of hands away from the body (belly button) centerline
- Eliminates any inward rotation of arms and ulnar deviation (outward turning of the hand to align the fingers to home row)
- Allows placement of the left and right keyboard halves to change arm outward/inward rotation
- Placement changes also allow
- Allows hand/wrist/arm kinetic variation for repetitive motions/postures reduction
- Fully successful in all applications
- Allows subtle but essential *minute* movement of the hand/wrist/arm aggregate minimizing static position changes with left or right keyboard section placement allowing subtle changes in posture and musculature activity
- Highly effective if used appropriately especially for inward arm rotation on a flat desktop especially for custom angulation or separation using an extended center connecting cord

SELECTED FYTR WEAPON TO CONQUER THE BYTR KEYBOARD

SECTION BB.2

The Goldtouch GTP-0044w Keyboard

www.goldtouch.com

Awareness Factor

The Goldtouch has unique infinitesimal adjustments in three "V" configuration planes (flat, tenting, angulation), for custom left and right-hand symmetrical positioning. An easily accessible angle change control encourages immediate and important variation of hand and wrist postures to prevent static loading and positioning. Wrist posture in both tented and flat "V" arrangements eliminates continual outward wrist bend (ulnar deviation) required on standard keyboards. Self- supporting symmetry is consistent with both tent shape and slope around the pivot ball. Note that beneficial adjustments can be small and very, very subtle.

FYTR FACTS

HOW THE GOLDTOUCH GTP-0044W REDUCES PAIN

SECTION BB.2.1

- Eliminates any pain triggered by hand pronation (palm downward facing) and ulnar deviation (outward turning of the hand to align the fingers to home row) from standard keyboards
- Infinite subtle but critical *minute* movement of dual plane angulation and immediate “lock-down” allows trials and analysis to determine most effective hand and wrist positioning
- If used with appropriate elbow or arm support, can fully address all forearm, hand and wrist static loading
- Placement and angulation changes also allow hand/wrist/arm kinetic variation to reduce repetitive motions/postures
- Fully successful in all “V” applications including when used as a flat but angled keyboard
- <u>Allows subtle but important</u> *minute* movement of the left or right keyboard sections at any time minimizing ongoing static hand/wrist/arm positioning relieving and changing static postures
- Highly effective when applied properly

SELECTED FYTR WEAPON TO CONQUER THE BYTR KEYBOARD

SECTION BB.2

The Kinesis Advantage Keyboard

www.kinesis-ergo.com

Awareness Factor

The Kinesis Advantage has full-size palm rests eliminating requirements for wrist rests or chair armrests. Keys set in curved depressions match relaxed finger contours reducing finger and hand action for keystrikes. Fully supported palms allow full hand and wrist relaxation, encouraging body neutral (straight) positioning.

Standard keyboards require outward hand rotation using weak small fingers to engage difficult-to-reach keys: (<enter>, <bksp>, <esc>, <tab>, <shift>). Remapping on the Advantage for thumb strike requires no deviation lessening potential overuse. Highly beneficial in relaxing hand and forearm musculature and keeping wrists straight directly addressing many RMI issues.

FYTR FACTS

HOW THE KINESIS ADVANTAGE REDUCES PAIN

SECTION BB.2.1

- Proper use of the palm rests fully supports hands, wrists, and forearms eliminating significant musculature effort
- With full hand and forearm support, shoulder relaxation naturally follows
- Keeps wrists and hands in body-neutral posture eliminating any ulnar deviation or, inward arm rotation required with a "V" hand configuration
- Often diminishes keyboarding discomfort without adjustments to standard Kinesis key layout
- Eliminates hand and arm inward rotation necessary for standard or "V" keyboards
- Inherent programming capability allows key remapping and moving to reduce identified finger or palm discomfort associated with striking specific keys or key combinations
- P programming capabilities also allow macros enabling one-touch key combinations reducing adverse finger postures
- Highly effective for reducing inward arm rotation caused by standard keyboards

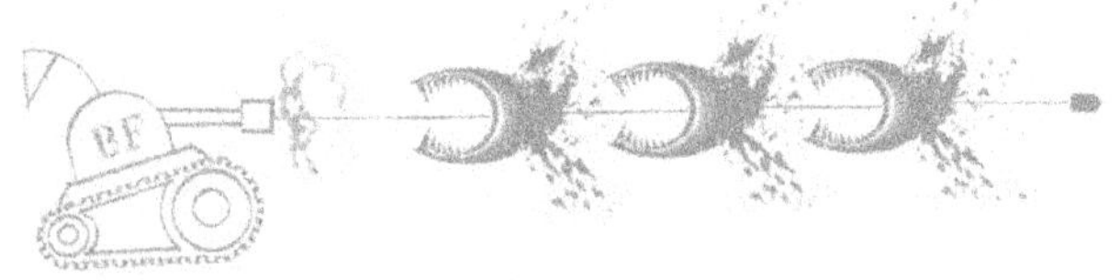
BF

CHAIR PAIN GENERATION

BYTR PAIN DEVICE #3

SECTION C

User Danger Level Rating

BYTR Pain Generation Potential: **High**
FYTR Alert Level: **High**
Recovery Potential Index: **Medium to High**

THE BYTR TASK CHAIR

SECTION C

Most users sit in an assigned or convenient chair with no appreciable thought as to the application or fit. The perfect computer task chair although highly desired is difficult to find.

Without specific attention to fit, the BYTRs have open pathways to cause pain. Shoes, clothing, and eyeglasses garner more attention to proper fit than most chairs.

Issues with common task chairs include:

- Lack of low back (lumbar) support
- Lack of upper back (thoracic) support
- Excessively high armrests
- Too deep a seat pan
- Inadequate seat adjustment height
- No scroll front edge
- Inadequate cushioning
- Many more

Chairs are well-known as a triggering device for high-level point pain, muscular strain, compressed nerves, etc. throughout the back–often with radicular pain down the legs and around the hips

BYTR TASK CHAIR OVERVIEW

SECTION C.1

Typical unadjustable chairs–high pain generators

Caution!
Any ("good") chair without combining other appropriate workstation elements can still force pain triggering postures

BYTR CHAIR PAIN SPECIFICS

INJURIES & SYMPTOMOLOGIES

SECTION C.2

C.2.1 Primary Targets of Pain & Injury

- Low back (lumbar spine)
- Upper back (thoracic spine)
- Neck (cervical spine)

C.2.2 Secondary Targets of Pain & Injury

- Legs
- Elbow

C.2.3 Destructive Capability Potential

- High trigger levels
- Muscle strain
- Neural compression
- Whole body ache

C.2.4 Symptomology

- Pain/Ache
- Numbness
- Tingling (sparks)
- Articulation sensory loss
- Contact stress/point pain

C.2.5 Symptomology levels

- Constant to severe (debilitating)

BYTR CHAIR PAIN DEVELOPMENT

INJURIES & SYMPTOMOLOGIES

SECTION C.3

Primary Anatomical Areas Affected

C.3.1 Low Back

- Forward lean–constant, leading to bulging disks or compressed nerves resulting in pain from a broad band across the back to radiating pain around the hips and down the back of the legs
- Side twisting–accessing files or work items also affects the entire low back, legs, and hips through racks as they exit the vertebral column
- Side bending–accessing low drawers or files also places pressure on the low back with similar pain patterns

C.3.2 Upper Back/Neck

- Forward lean forces constant firing of mid-back musculature with a subsequent strain in the large muscle groups and the small postural muscles
- Head extension–looking up to view monitor from a forward leaning torso continually fires the upper back and neck musculature leading to muscle strain and subsequent neural compression in the upper back

BYTR CHAIR PAIN DEVELOPMENT

INJURIES & SYMPTOMOLOGIES

SECTION C.4

Secondary Anatomical Areas Affected

C.4.1 Legs & Feet

- Forward lean compresses femoral triangle vasculature and neural pathways causing neural compression and vascular constriction into the legs causing numbness or pain
- Forward lean causes sciatic nerve stretching through the gluteal area causing pain, numbness or tingling

C.4.2 Elbow

- Elbows can continually strike the armrests (due to ill-fitting/configuration) causing impact trauma with constant irritation-especially noted at (outside) lateral epicondyle with elbows held inside the armrests and at (inside) medial epicondyle with arms held outside of the armrest
- Continual "leaning" on the elbows on the armrests, continual bruising occurs with constant irritation with potential cubital tunnel irritation impacting the ulnar nerve with associated pain at the bottom of the elbow sometimes tracking through the ulnar nerve along the edge of the arm to the small finger

CHAIR
FYTR
WEAPONS

**SELECTED WEAPONS TO
FIGHT & CONQUER
THE BYTR CHAIR**

**KNOWN TO BE
HIGHLY EFFECTIVE
FOR
REDUCING PAIN & INJURY**

Neutral Posture Task Chair

FYTR Rating Scale

Pain Reduction from Mouse Use: **High**
Fytr Rating Scale: **High**
Recovery Index: **High**

THE NEUTRAL POSTURE TASK CHAIR

SECTION CC

www.neutralposture.com

Awareness Factor

A highly adjustable computer task chair is a major FYTR Device addressing many unknown and unrecognized postural problems.

Many computer task chairs, advertised as being "Ergonomic" fall well short. Understanding the nuances and details of specific brands and applications is ***THE*** main element in any FYTRs toolbox. ***Application is key,*** *application to body size, body shape, injury triggers and work methods.*

Most users view the chair as only a device to rest on as an alternative to standing. For short-term sitting, a simple box, stool or even rock may suffice.

THE NEUTRAL POSTURE TASK CHAIR

The technology explosion shackles users to computer workstations for most or even exceeding entire workdays. Dr. James Levine, of the Mayo Clinic, coined the term “sitting is the new smoking,” showing long-term sitting is hazardous to user health. Only lately has this concept become mainstream, however, few really understand it or can make remedies.

Often seen is a highly adjustable chair misused or placed within a poorly designed workstation. The result is a weak solution or a poor proactive approach to existing or developing injuries or conditions.

It is paramount with any good chair that the user is adequately trained on its use, especially in the subtle adjustments specific to their individual anatomical requirements, and the reasons it works for them.

Understand, comfort is not the issue; non-pain is. User understanding of the approach is all important as are the principles of recovery and proactive preventions of injuries and pain.

Remember posture change is **beneficial,** especially in subtle increments, characteristic of a good chair.

HOW THE NEUTRAL POSTURE TASK CHAIR REDUCES PAIN

SECTION CC.1

- Highly adjustable in all planes of body support
- Allows full relaxation and support of body musculature
- Customizable to a vast majority of body styles and types
- Interchangeable parts allow complete customization to varying anatomical dimensions
- Highly adjustable in back angulation and height for full back support
- Air bladder to articulate any custom low back spine curvature
- Seat depth adjustment allowing clearance for popliteal crease behind the knee
- Seat tilt adjustment allows control of pelvic tilt addressing lumbar plexus neural track compression and gluteal area stretch
- Interchangeable shocks of varying length allow specific height adjustment above floor level to address lower leg dimensions
- Three-axis adjustable armrests control arm resting posture
- Adjustable and removable armrests eliminate sources of impact trauma to the medial, lateral or ventral elbow

TASK CHAIR FYTR FACTS

SECTION CC.1.2

- Often perceived as being a cure-all for all back symptomology–it is not
- Proper keyboard, mouse and monitor positioning is required with an appropriate chair to address all symptomology involving upper, mid and low back issues
- Eliminate extended reach and forward lean to enable users full use of supportive contoured chair back
- Proper fit required as determined by analysis to be effective
- Without proper fit and application, symptomology can worsen
- Improper posture in a good chair will continue if not worsen symptomology
- An appropriate chair will negate the use of a footrest
- Improper attention to the subtleties of chair usage or adjustments can inadvertently worsen specific injuries over time
- Encourages the subtle but essential *minute* adjustment of overall body segment relationships
- *With sit-stand workstations an inappropriate chair can worsen pain, negating the sit-stand benefits*

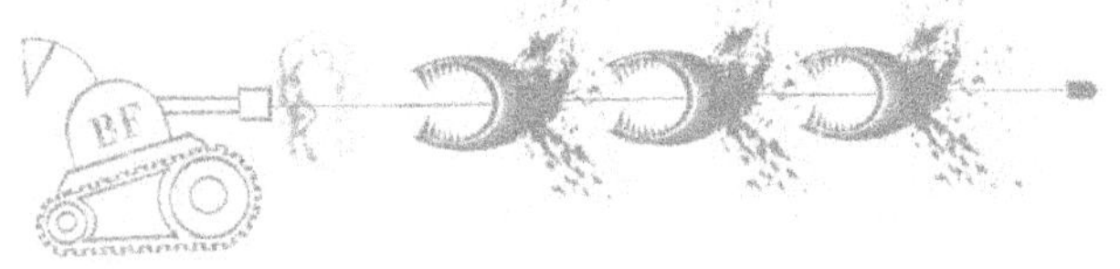
BF

MONITOR
&
LINE-OF-SIGHT
PAIN
GENERATION

BYTR PAIN
DEVICE #4

SECTION D

User Danger Level Rating

BYTR Pain Generation Potential**: High**
FYTR Alert Level: **High**
Recovery Potential Index**: Medium to High**

THE BYTR MONITOR OVERVIEW

SECTION D.1

The computer monitor and associated sightlines are the main visual connections between Humans, computer devices and work task reference material. Definitively contributory to potential high-level pain, these cause eye, neck, and upper back strain. Temporary blindness has been documented as a medical phenomenon under specific conditions.

100% monitor usage occurs when mousing, keyboarding, or voice activating. Highly used in many professions, it has now become a known tool for BYTR activities.

Pain and injury stem mostly result from constant activation of the neck, upper back, shoulder musculature (static loading/posturing) and especially the small muscles in the eye sockets.

Mild to severe headaches result from this continual visual contact with the monitor screen. Associated strained head positions during input and/or reference activities (reference material position, AKA line-of-sight) are also contributory.

Continual visual contact with the monitor and improper sight lines provides more opportunity for the BYTRs *and* the higher the risk for pain with loss of focus and productivity.

BYTR MONITOR OVERVIEW–CON'T

SECTION D.1.1

Typical monitor with no specific or useful means of distance, height or angulation adjustment as a high pain generator

Default stand supplied with monitor–monitors are rarely repositioned on desktops, sacrificing proper distance-of-focus and lines-of-sight (when referencing documents)

Pain and discomfort generated by the monitor are often confused with pain and discomfort generated by the chair or keyboard positioning.

Detailed observation and biomechanical analysis are required to determine the actual pain generators. Eliminate one source before moving on to analyze the next area of discomfort.

BYTR MONITOR FYTR FACTS

SECTION D.1.2

- Monitors are largely associated with eye strain and highly contributory to neck, shoulder, and back pain
- Allowing clearance of the desktop surface area for work tasks or keyboard and mouse, monitors are commonly pushed to the far desk edge
- The concept of a moveable (position changing) monitor to change focal distance and overall back posture is generally unknown, misunderstood, uninstalled or under-utilized
- Gross monitor movement on desktop rarely considered or performed
- Subtle height adjustments rarely used to bring monitors to appropriate focal distance
- Most observed height adjustments are books, paper reams and cardboard boxes
- Monitor base occupies valuable desktop real estate
- The concept of dedicated computer glasses is generally unknown with off-the-shelf units available to address contributory elements to eye strain and irritation such as glare or air movement–however not applicable for all users or all conditions

BYTR MONITOR PAIN SPECIFICS

INJURIES & SYMPTOMOLOGIES

SECTION D.1.3

D.1.3.1 Primary Targets of Pain & Injury

- Neck
- Shoulders
- Eyes

D.1.3.2 Secondary Targets of Pain & Injury

- Upper Back
- Low Back

D.1.3.3 Destructive Capability Potential

- High trigger levels
- Muscle strain/sprain
- Nerve compression

D.1.3.4 Symptomology

- Large Area Pain/Ache
- Shoulder/upper arm numbness

D.1.3.5 Symptomology levels

- Constant to severe (debilitating)
- Minimally annoying

BYTR MONITOR PAIN DEVELOPMENT

BODY AREAS & CAUSES

SECTION D.1.4

Primary Pain Area Specifics

D.1.4.1 Neck

- Constant head forward posture with neck extended (head tilted upwards) places constant loads on the neck and upper back musculature ("overuse" syndrome)
- Tight musculature from constant loads also compresses neural tracks with resultant pain

D.1.4.2 Shoulders

- Associated "overuse" of upper shoulder muscles
- Shoulders often held in inward rotation at forward lean, closing the angle between upper arm and forearm with continued tension and pain

D.1.4.3 Head

- Constant tight upper back muscles compress nerve pathways triggering pain
- Associated pain often travels upwards through neck inducing severe headaches

D.1.4.4 Eyes

- Eye muscles must constantly correct (static loading) from incorrect sight lines / focal distance resulting in eye strain

BYTR MONITOR PAIN DEVELOPMENT

BODY AREAS & CAUSES

SECTION D.1.5

Secondary Pain Area Specifics

D.1.5.1 Upper Back

- Monitors at the far side of desktop inadvertently pulls user closer for in-focus viewing causing forward lean
- Forward lean separates user back from chair backrest resulting in static loading of upper back musculature having the potential to compress upper back nerve paths (brachial plexus) in upper back resulting in continual low-level pain (among other maladies)

D.1.5.2 Low Back

- The forward lean also has similar effects on low backs with non-support from chair backrest
- Monitor and improper sight lines can have far-reaching causation to low back potential or imminent spinal column disk issues

BYTR LINE-OF-SIGHT OVERVIEW

SECTION D.2

Computer users often place reference documents flat on the desktop with the monitor oriented vertically. Attempting to place documents in a near vertical position alongside the monitor, users often install inexpensive A-frame styles or, holders on raised stands.

With these, differing sight lines and focus distance result, forcing repeated head and eye movement. Potential high-level pain, such as neck and upper back strain can develop. The tiny eye socket muscles are especially affected, commonly known as eye strain.

Also, the non-varying overall user posture from continuous monitor or document viewing places continual (static) activation on the overall back and shoulder muscle groups (unless adequately supported).

Strained head positions combined with constant visual activity can develop pain normally not associated with monitor or document viewing. These adverse postures provide more opportunity for the BYTRs, compromising focus and productivity.

BYTR LINE-OF-SIGHT OVERVIEW
CON'T

SECTION D.2.1

Typical posture when referencing material on a flat desktop forcing neck flexion static loading as a high pain generator in addition to monitor viewing issues

Repetitive twisting is a causal relationship to neck and eye strain forcing repetitive action of eye musculature as the distance-of-focus between monitor and reference material changes

Pain and discomfort generated by a poor line-of-sight and distance-of-focus are often ignored, misunderstood or confused with pain and discomfort generated by the chair or keyboard positioning.

The pain issues stemming from the monitor and poor sight lines are similar but distinct. Solving one does not guarantee solving the other. Eliminate one source before moving on to analyze the other by analyzing and solving both independently.

BYTR LINE-OF-SIGHT FYTR FACTS

SECTION D.2.2

- Line-of-sight and focus distance are often unknown or dismissed as a pain triggers
- Poor focus distance contributes significantly to eye strain
- Improper line-of-sight and focus distance from monitors and document holders are also highly responsible for neck, shoulder, and back pain
- The concept of adjusting monitor or document holders to improve focus distance and overall back posture is mostly unknown, misunderstood, under used or cumbersome to implement
- Gross monitor or document holder movement on desktop rarely considered
- Typical document holder (inexpensive "A-frame" type) is generally the only option considered for implementation
- Employ subtle and correct document placement to establish an appropriate line-of-sight and focus distance for the monitor
- Off-the-shelf eyeglasses are available to address contributory elements to eye strain and irritation such as glare or air movement–however not applicable for all users or conditions

BYTR LINE-OF-SIGHT PAIN SPECIFICS

INJURIES & SYMPTOMOLOGIES

SECTION D.2.3

D.2.3.1 Primary Targets of Pain & Injury

- Neck
- Shoulders
- Eyes

D.2.3.2 Secondary Targets of Pain & Injury

- Upper Back
- Low Back

D.2.3.3 Destructive Capability Potential

- High trigger levels
- Muscle strain/sprain
- Neural network compression
- Air passages constriction
- Neck vasculature constriction

D.2.3.4 Symptomology

- Large Area Pain/Ache
- Shoulder/upper arm numbness
- Overall fatigue

D.2.3.5 Symptomology levels

- Constant to severe (debilitating)
- Minimally triggers continual annoyance

BYTR LINE-OF-SIGHT PAIN DEVELOPMENT

BODY AREAS & CAUSES

SECTION D.2.4

Primary Pain Area Specifics

D.2.4.1 Neck

- Constant head forward posture with neck flexed (tilted downwards) places static loads on the neck and upper back
- Tight musculature from continual head flexion, extension or twisting also compresses nerve pathways and air passages
- Repetitive head twisting and flexion from poorly located document holder adversely affects neck musculature

D.2.4.2 Shoulders

- Closing the angle between upper arm and forearm during forward lean, places shoulder musculature in static loading generating pain and discomfort

D.2.4.3 Eyes

- Eye muscles must continually activate to correct from an improper line-of-sight or focus distance resulting in overuse of eye musculature (strain)

BYTR LINE-OF-SIGHT PAIN DEVELOPMENT

BODY AREAS & CAUSES

SECTION D.2.5

Secondary Pain Area Specifics

D.2.5.1 Upper Back

- Forward lean results with documents placed on flat desktops pulling users closer for viewing or adequate reading especially with small detail print causing forward lean
- Forward lean separates user backs from chair backrests resulting in continual activation of upper back musculature with potential to compress upper back nerve pathways (brachial plexus) resulting in continual low to high-level pain
- Head twist also affects large upper back musculature with asymmetrical loading

D.2.5.2 Low Back

- The forward lean also has similar effects on low backs with non-support from chair backrest
- Monitor and improper sight lines are a definitive but subtle source for low back potential or imminent spinal column disk issues

MONITOR & LINES-OF-SIGHT

FYTR WEAPONS

KNOWN TO BE
HIGHLY EFFECTIVE
FOR
REDUCING PAIN & INJURY

SECTION DD

FYTR Rating Scale

Pain Reduction from non- adjustable monitor usage: **High**
Fytr Rating Scale: **High**
Recovery Index: **High**

THE MONITOR ARM OVERVIEW

SECTION DD.1

The monitor arm has many hidden and obvious benefits as an effective proactive and relatively unknown FRIENDLY or FYTR Device.

Most users only accept the typical attached (but removable) unadjustable base, as the only means of monitor support.

When replacing the standard base, arm usage will free up valuable desktop real estate.

Wide-ranging viewing angle, plane-of-focus, and line-of-sight are easily adapted to specific individual needs. These adjustments (with an attached handle) are available continuously and immediately dependent on need or discomfort (posture, biomechanics, eye fatigue).

An excellent functional monitor (assembly) includes ease-of-use positioning with immediate height, depth, and tilt changeability in all planes without requiring cumbersome manual loosening and tightening of backside adjusting screws, knobs or cranks.

THE SPACECO MONITOR ARM

SECTION DD.1.1

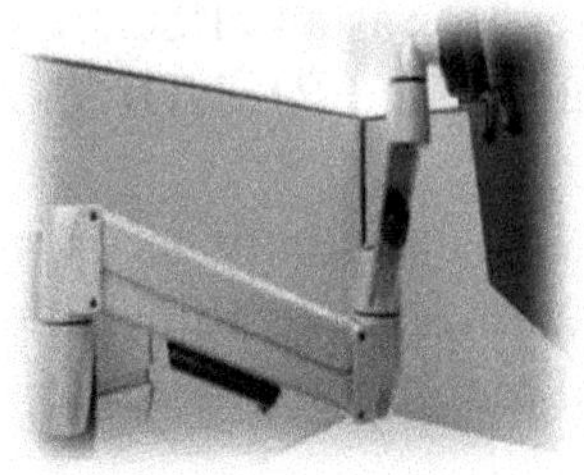

www.spaceco.com

Awareness Factor

The SpaceCo Monitor Arm should be seen as a major FYTR Device as it addresses many unknown and unrecognized postural problems.

Astonishingly, lack of a monitor arm can completely negate all beneficial elements of an otherwise well set-up workstation. Without a monitor arm, even a good chair is rendered useless by a continual forward lean to view a distant monitor.

Primary benefits include easy continual and essential minute viewing adjustments allowing users to place neck and back musculature into beneficial relaxed non-injuring positions.

HOW THE SPACECO MONITOR ARM REDUCES PAIN

SECTION DD.1.2

- Allows immediate and proper placement of monitor for custom focus distance
- Eliminates forward lean for adequate focusing on the monitor screen
- Allows users to use chair backrests addressing many back issues
- Eliminates the need for neck extension associated with the forward lean
- Allows vertical positioning addressing neck posture and viewing angle
- Horizontal placement minimizes head twisting during document/data sourcing using an appropriate document holder

SPACECO MONITOR ARM FYTR FACTS

SECTION DD.1.3

- Allows a significant variation with eye focus distance and varying eyeball muscle tension minimizing static positioning
- Highly effective in eliminating associated muscle strain in the neck, shoulders, upper back and especially eyes
- Highly effective as a proactive approach
- Quick release minimizes adverse lifting back postures when moving monitors to different workstations

THE DOCUMENT HOLDER

OVERVIEW

SECTION DD.2

Often dismissed as a simple unsophisticated desk accessory, document holders have many under-utilized and hidden benefits.

Common document holders are often a simple stand-up "A-frame" placed on the desk surface next to monitors or a small platform on a stand. Others are simple single sheet holder held by a clip attached to the monitor by an extending arm.

The overall benefit of a desktop "A-frame" holder is in raising reference documents from the flat desktop to a more easily readable upright position. This removes significant strain on neck and shoulder musculature. Placed alongside the monitor, this style still requires repeated head twisting to view both the holder and the monitor. Positioning a holder directly in front of the monitor for a correct line-of-sight viewing, forces the monitor further away from the front desk edge and the user, creating focus plane issues.

Small hanging (from the monitor) document holders have one or two page limitations. Large documents or books require a flat desktop or a large substantial holder.

THE VU-RYTE DOCUMENT HOLDER

SECTION DD.2.1

www.vuryte.com

Awareness Factor

Directly attached to the monitor, the Vu Ryte VR59GR and VR79GR Document Holders are major, albeit subtle FYTR Devices addressing many unknown and unrecognized postural issues.

Both units place documents in a direct line (of sight) orientation to the monitor allowing proper focus distance. The “drop-down” adjustability of the document easel or platform exploits the desktop front edge, a heretofore under-utilized area. By bringing the reference material and monitor over the front desk edge, and when using an under-desk keyboard tray or a lap desk, users can sit back fully against the chair backrest, attaining full back support benefitting any low back, upper back, and neck tight musculature. Larger platforms for books, large documents or writing subtly reduce adverse extended reach postures required on flat desktops.

HOW THE VU-RYTE DOCUMENT HOLDER REDUCES PAIN

SECTION DD.2.2

- Places both reference material and monitor in an identical line-of-sight and focus distance
- Eliminates the forced forward lean and repetitive head twisting for viewing and focusing on both monitor screen and reference material
- Proper placement allows full use of chair backrest addressing many back issues
- Eliminates the need for neck flexion from using reference material on a flat desktop
- Highly effective in minimizing head movement from body-neutral, when viewing documents and monitor repeatedly, eliminating associated muscle strain in neck, shoulders, upper back and especially eyes

VU-RYTE DOCUMENT HOLDER FYTR FACTS

SECTION DD.2.3

- Removing the document platform from the mounting frame provides a convenient handle allowing quick and easy monitor adjustments for important subtle chair posture or focus distance changes
- Proactive for body-neutral positioning

FOOTREST PAIN GENERATION

BYTR PAIN DEVICE #5

SECTION E

User Danger Level Rating

BYTR Pain Generation Potential: **High**
FYTR Alert Level: **High**
Recovery Potential Index: **Medium to High**

THE BYTR FOOTREST OVERVIEW

SECTION E

Inappropriate application of footrests generates significant pain. Often mistakenly supplied by unskilled practitioners, these will make a bad situation worse.

An optimal workstation should not require a footrest. However, users having definite lower extremity issues or have a short knee to heel dimension, requiring special foot support. For example, children usually need one when sitting in adult chairs.

An improper and static foot positioning during long workdays triggers ankle strain. Too extreme of an extended foot (toes pointed) affects calf musculature.

Horizontal bars and shelf edges used for footrests on counter level (42") height workstations place users feet on a sharp edge or in harmful positions for long periods. This continual and specific pressure contact on the foot soles may cause maladies such as Morton's Neuroma. Peripheral neuropathy or circulatory conditions (diabetes) are at risk without proper footrest use and application. High chair or stool foot rings force adverse leg and total body posture, triggering or exacerbating new or existing pain.

BYTR FOOTREST OVERVIEW–CON'T

SECTION E.1

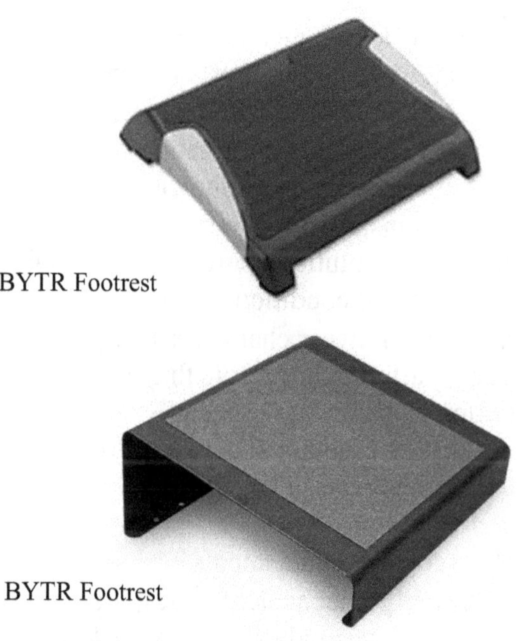

BYTR Footrest

BYTR Footrest

Awareness Factor

To address any foot, leg, ankle or posture issue, a precise analysis must precede any footrest application, as footrest use or non-use affects the entire postural chain. A typical fixed angle unadjustable unit is dysfunctional for a vast majority of discomfort issues-unless applicable for a specific condition or situation.

FOOTREST FYTR FACTS

SECTION E.1.2

- A familiar love-hate relationship exists between users and footrests in general
- Proper footrest application must consider common erroneous information or lack of authentic (practitioner) knowledge
- Footrests installed without a definitive direction or solution approach, often make a problematic condition worse
- Consider footwear characteristics (high heels, platform shoes, sole thickness, friction coefficients- especially with sneakers and leather shoe soles) for proper footrest application
- Footrests should garner equal attention as other workstation elements
- Differing biomechanical issues, identified by a definitive analysis require rocking or non-rocking foot rest styles
- Footrest applications involve the entire anatomical chain including body parts far away from the feet (such as the wrists) from lesser known or less obvious remote relationships
- The optimum workstation should not require a footrest allowing feet flat on the floor-sitting or standing
- Not all users are in need of a footrest

BYTR FOOTREST PAIN SPECIFICS

INJURIES & SYMPTOMOLOGIES

SECTION E.1.3

E.1.3.1 Primary Targets of Pain & Injury
- Feet
- Ankles

E.1.3.2 Secondary Targets of Pain & Injury
- Knees
- Legs
- Hips

E.1.3.3 Destructive Capability Potential
- High trigger levels
- Tarsal tunnel syndrome
- Morton's neuroma
- Tendinitis
- Tenosynovitis
- Muscle strain/sprain

E.1.3.4 Symptomology
- Pain/Ache
- Numbness
- Tingling (sparks)
- Articulation sensory loss
- Contact stress/point pain

E.1.3.5 Symptomology levels
- Constant to severe (debilitating)

BYTR FOOTREST PAIN DEVELOPMENT

INJURIES & SYMPTOMOLOGIES

SECTION E.1.4

Primary Areas

E.1.4.1 Feet

- Vasculature constriction from improper or static leg positioning can cause numbness and pain also promoting associated circulatory problems
- Static foot posture can compress neural pathways resulting in foot numbness

E.1.4.2 Lower Leg/Ankle/Feet

- Flexed foot (pointed down) continually contracts the calf muscle (gastrocnemius) with potential muscle cramps or spasms, especially if the angle between torso and leg is less than 90° compromising blood flow
- Unadjustable or stationary footrest styles especially affect users with leg and foot circulation issues (diabetics)

BYTR FOOTREST PAIN DEVELOPMENT

INJURIES & SYMPTOMOLOGIES

SECTION E.1.5

Secondary Areas

E.1.5.1 Back & Neck

- Lack of a footrest forces forward lean with a bent head, forcing leg dangle and knee lowering while sitting on an (excessively) deep seat pan pulling the users back away from the chair backrest placing back and neck musculature into static loading

E.1.5.2 Knees

- An excessively high footrest a strain knees worsening existing knee issues

E.1.5.3 Hips

- When knees are higher than the front chair edge from an (excessively) high footrest, hips can subtly revert into a constant outward rotation and adversely affect the hip joint resulting in minor irritations
- High knees compresses the femoral triangle limiting neural sensations or vasculature flow causing numbness and tingling down the frontal legs

FOOTREST FYTR WEAPONS

KNOWN TO BE HIGHLY EFFECTIVE FOR REDUCING PAIN & INJURY

FYTR Ratings

Pain Reduction from improper or no footrest usage: **High**

Fytr Rating Scale: **High**

Recovery Index: **High**

THE FOX BAY FOOTREST

SECTION EE

The typical footrest is another relatively unknown BYTR Device with a mistaken belief it "rests the foot," as it effects are unrecognized and its use often misplaced. Any lower extremity discomfort is often inaccurately believed solvable with the application of a footrest.

Looked upon as an afterthought or simple accessory, a properly applied footrest can be an active FYTR Weapon.

A detailed biomechanical analysis is necessary to determine the most applicable footrest. Footrest usage science lacks the knowledge depth of other computer workstation devices.

The footrest can be a dependable ally when subtle symptomologies appear in the user's legs, ankles or feet. Choose well one with adjustable height and an adjustable angle allowing the rocking of ankles and feet, becoming self-adjusting to footwear and individual preferences. Occasionally investigation will require a custom unit development with a specific foot angle and height to address unique postural requirements.

The key is not just a footrest, but an appropriate one.

THE FOX BAY FOOTREST

SECTION EE.1

Self-adjusting/rocking model to accommodate user individual requirements

Height adjustable model allowing significant support when required

Awareness Factor

The footrest should be viewed as a significant FYTR Weapon as it addresses many unknown, unrecognized and overlooked postural problems.

Lack of an appropriate footrest can negate many beneficial elements of a well set-up workstation. Optimally a footrest should not be required. An optimal workstation allows feet placed flat on the floor (respective of footwear) with a footrest applicable only to specialized conditions.

When required, configure the footrest specifically with the user's body position, dimensions, and (if any) unique anatomical requirements. Continually neglected is ensuring the feet are in full contact with the footwear inner soles.

HOW THE FOX BAY FOOTREST REDUCES PAIN

SECTION EE.1.2

- Adjustable angulation models allow custom angulation of foot addressing specific pain or posture triggers
- Rocking motion allows unconscious foot flexion and extension for foot, ankle or lower leg musculature or vasculature continued motion
- Prevents foot dangle when high desk forces high chair seat level resulting in unsupported feet forcing compression in the popliteal crease (area behind knee containing neural and vasculature tracks)
- Allows variance of single or dual legs and feet if used as an occasional step to raise leg for change in musculature action and overall positioning provided normal seated posture is with both feet flat on the floor
- Eliminates the chair starbase used as a foot rest compressing popliteal crease and inadvertently pulling torso forward potentially triggering back or leg issues
- Height adjustable models allow high-level support for the knee, leg and foot therapy and an optional "leg stretch" when desired

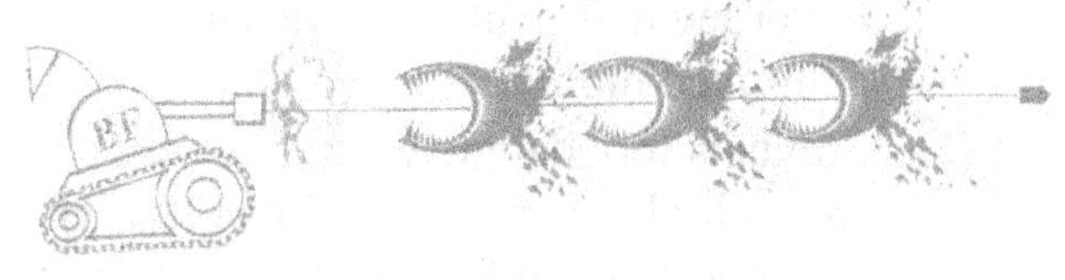

HIGH DESKTOP PAIN GENERATION

BYTR PAIN DEVICE #6

SECTION F

User Danger Level Rating

BYTR Pain Generation Potential: **High**
FYTR Alert Level: **High**
Recovery Potential Index: **Medium to High**

THE BYTR HIGH DESKTOP

SECTION F

Many computer workstations comprise a keyboard, mouse, and monitor placed on a typical 30-inch high flat surface, considered a "high desk." Positioning computer devices, including laptops, on such high surfaces force users to raise arms and hands for keyboard and mouse engagement or handwriting. With no adequate support the upper extremity musculature fatigues, eventually leading to pain.

Many users mistake shoulder and arm symptomology as caused by something other than high desk keyboard or mouse positioning. This appears logical since the hands, fingers, and arms perform all actionable input tasks.

It is this mistaken pain origin that allows BYTRs the opportunity to attack. Applications of erroneous or "voodoo" ergonomics without attention to this critical workstation element results in open invitations for BYTRs.

The high desk pain origins are subtle, involving misdirection. Simple off-the-shelf purchases are ineffective. Only a real analysis and observation with proper applications combined with all other workstation equipment will solve these camouflaged pains.

BYTR HIGH DESKTOP OVERVIEW

SECTION F.1

Observe these postures to determine the effect of high desktops

Typical high desktop with laptop having contributory elements to pain and injury

Awareness Factor

Users often place laptop computers on standard workstation surfaces, whether an office cubicle, home desk, kitchen countertop or dining table. In using the laptop keyboard a subtle, extended reach, dropped elbows and unsupported back postures result (see above),

Using a standard PC, keyboard use also occurs on the high desktop with the same issues.Lowering of both the keyboard and mouse height is the primary FYTR Weapon to address these issues of the high desktop.

BYTR HIGH DESKTOP FYTR FACTS

SECTION F.1.2

- Another relatively unknown and unrecognized pain generator as over time the desk has defaulted into a 30" high-level
- Thought to be an "ideal" level for an effective seated work position having with arm support while using pen and paper
- Old-fashioned secretary desks had side "returns" three inches below desk level to orient the large typewriter keyboard to a lower level seated position
- The computer keyboard default placement became the high desktop as it did not have the mass of a typewriter requiring a lower surface
- The current 30" high desktops with higher level keyboards force users to arm flex (closing up the angle between the forearm and upper arm), or force extended reach for keyboard and mouse access
- Importantly, a sit-stand adjustable height workstations should NOT be confused with a high desktop (defined as a stationary non- adjustable height work surface)

BYTR HIGH DESKTOP PAIN SPECIFICS

INJURIES & SYMPTOMOLOGIES

SECTION F.1.3

F.1.3.1 Primary Targets of Pain & Injury

- Shoulders
- Forearms

F.1.3.2 Secondary Targets of Pain & Injury

- Hands
- Wrists
- Elbow

F.1.3.3 Destructive Capability Potential

- High trigger levels
- Muscle strain
- Neural network compression

F.1.3.4 Symptomology

- Pain/Ache
- Shoulder/upper arm numbness

F.1.3.5 Symptomology levels

- Constant to severe (debilitating)
- Minimally annoying

BYTR HIGH DESKTOP PAIN DEVELOPMENT

INJURIES & SYMPTOMOLOGIES

SECTION F.1.4

Primary Areas

F.1.4.1 Shoulders

- Forces inward rotation of mousing arm/shoulder into static loading/positioning to engage the mouse or keyboard
- Often forces asymmetrical back positioning with the lowering or dipping of the mousing shoulder when the opposing arm is resting on a chair armrest serving only as a leaning support

F.1.4.2 Forearms

- Extended reach forces static loading of forearm musculature throughout computing time with a resultant strain

Secondary Areas

F.1.4.3 Hands, Wrists, Elbow

- With associated extended reach, high-desk level mouse manipulation forces "waving hello" and "goodbye" action on wrists (see mouse section)
- Extended reach also places torsion on elbow joint with a resultant ligament strain

HIGH DESKTOP FYTR WEAPONS

KNOWN TO BE HIGHLY EFFECTIVE FOR REDUCING PAIN & INJURY

FYTR Rating Scale

Pain Reduction from high desktop usage: **High**
Fytr Rating Scale: **High**
Recovery Index: **High**

THE UNDER-DESK KEYBOARD TRAY

SECTION FF

This is a highly versatile FYTR Device to address significant arm, shoulder, and back pain. Often uninstalled, as many desks have an underdesk central pencil drawer, perceived as too important to remove. In actuality when a pencil drawer is inventoried, its importance is revealed as less than necessary.

Often an ordinary surface such as a kitchen table or countertop serves as a laptop or notebook computer workstation, negating any possibility of a keyboard tray installation. Therefore, a wireless keyboard and mouse used on a lapdesk (as a low-level keyboard tray) enables a more supported back position or posture.

When used with an appropriate chair, this combination will provide a high-level of body-neutral in lowering the hand/arm aggregate allowing opportunity for a fully supported back. To fully address any seated posture on any typical high desk, a keyboard tray is essential, with the alternative being a wireless keyboard (for PCs or laptops) held in creative (lap) positions. The mouse must accompany the keyboard to the tray and NOT remain on the high desktop, eliminating all extended reach.

THE UNDER-DESK KEYBOARD TRAY

SECTION FF.1

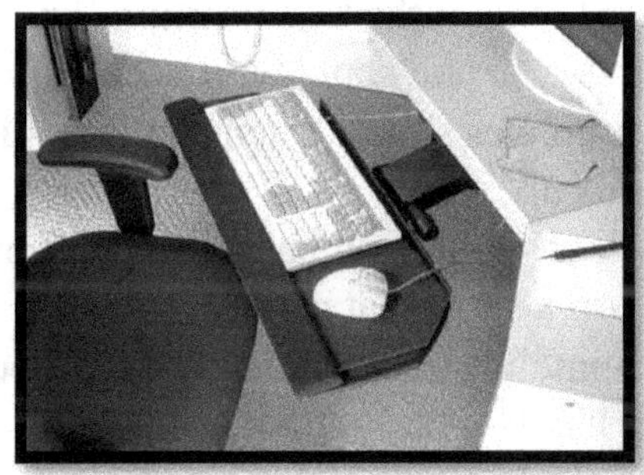

Awareness Factor

The Under-desk Keyboard Tray is a major FYTR Device addressing many unknown and unrecognized postural problems.

Lack of a tray will negate any of the beneficial elements of a well set up workstation. When combined with other Friendly Devices, the tray will do much to eliminate a vast majority of known static and dynamic loaded musculature, also allowing additional (albeit subtle) arm and torso adjustments for full body-neutral positioning.

HOW THE UNDER-DESK KEYBOARD TRAY REDUCES PAIN

SECTION FF.1.1

- Allows the lowering of hands to near lap level, one of the best positions known to relax arm and shoulder musculature
- Eliminates shoulder tension in holding arms up
- Allows a full lean back into chair backrest (with a short seat pan)
- Minutely adjusts tilt angle for proper line up hands with forearms
- Brings hand down for mousing eliminating excessive mouse grip
- Encourages overall relaxed computer posture when combined with other Friendly Devices in a workstation

KEYBOARD TRAY FYTR FACT

SECTION FF.3

- A negative platform tilt (tilting downward away from the torso) is paramount for complete appropriate application
- A lateral slide action is also a little-known FYTR Device that addresses inward arm rotation, addressing subtle shoulder issues
- Highly necessary for a complete and correctly set up computer workstation

THE WASTEBASKET PAIN GENERATION

BYTR PAIN DEVICE #7

SECTION G

FYTR Rating Scale

BYTR Pain Generation Potential: **High**
FYTR Alert Level: **High**
Recovery Potential Index: **Medium to High**

THE BYTR WASTEBASKET

SECTION G

Wastebaskets inhabit every workstation and are one of the sneakiest and misunderstood BYTR Devices. Found in desk footwells, they conspire with recreational gear, lunch, shopping goods, and other items to consume valuable underdesk leg space, allowing the BYTRs to attack the low back, hips, and legs.

This assemblage of personal paraphernalia remains innocuous, well camouflaged and virtually ignored. This occupation and crowding of prime underdesk real estate force users to twist their waist and hips to find alternative leg clearance, removing the lower extremities from a body-neutral relaxed posture.

This continual (static) twisting, when held for long periods, affects all back, hip and upper leg musculature with potential strain, sprain, vasculature, and neural constriction and pain

Forcing lower body accommodation into adverse postures presents a high risk for pain development.

BYTR WASTEBASKET OVERVIEW

SECTION G.1

Deep in the abyss of many desk footwells…

There exists a relatively unknown and unrecognized BYTR Device. Highly efficient it can fool even the best BYTR FYTR

BYTR WASTEBASKET BYTR FACTS

SECTION G.1.2

- The wastebasket is a relatively unknown and overlooked BYTR Device
- The wastebasket has a subtle but significant impact on many other body parts (especially when the forced twist position is constant)
- Users and BYTR FYTRs often overlook the forced twist as a pain contributor
- Wastebaskets will often exacerbate an ongoing or developing back problem– especially when twisting, posture or tasks directly contribute to existing at-risk conditions
- There is no requirement for installing a FYTR Device since the actual workstation reconfiguration is the optimum solution requiring little or no effort
- A subtle twist can trigger muscular strain, vasculature compression, or neural impingement and are uncovered by in-depth observation and analysis

BYTR WASTEBASKET PAIN SPECIFICS

INJURIES & SYMPTOMOLOGIES

SECTION G.1.3

G.1.3.1 Primary Targets of Pain & Injury

- Low Back
- Hips/Upper Leg

G.1.3.2 Secondary Targets of Pain & Injury

- Shoulder
- Lower Leg/Ankle

G.1.3.3 Destructive Capability Potential

- High trigger levels
- Muscle strain
- Vasculature constriction
- Neural compression

G.1.3.4 Symptomology

- Pain/Ache
- Numbness
- Tingling (sparks)

G.1.3.5 Symptomology levels

- Constant to severe (debilitating)

BYTR WASTEBASKET PAIN

DEVELOPMENT

INJURIES & SYMPTOMOLOGIES

SECTION G.1.4

G.1.4.1 Low Back

- Low back musculature pain results from forced twisting with the legs angled from the torso to avoid wastebaskets and other under-desk clutter
- Continued adverse static positioning held at length from bad positioning
- Constant low-level pain and ache are common
- Muscle strain and adverse effects on spinal column affect disc issues and neural root compression can result in high-level pain
- Contributory to other body area pain such as upper and mid back

G.1.4.2 Hips/Upper Leg

- Forced twist causes muscle tightness and compression of neural roots, which enervate hip and gluteal musculature (sciatica)
- Typical constant overall low-level ache and pain flares in the lower extremities as adverse positioning affects a significant amount of torso and leg musculature

BYTR WASTEBASKET

PAIN DEVELOPMENT

INJURIES & SYMPTOMOLOGIES –CON'T

SECTION G.1.5

Secondary Anatomical Areas

G.1.5.1 Shoulder

- Body twist to the right can pull mousing shoulder back forcing a right hand or arm extended reach to engage mouse and keyboard
- Left twist can force holding mousing hand in outward rotation from body

G.1.5.2 Lower Leg/Ankle/Feet

- Continual twist compresses vasculature and nerves between torso and legs
- Lack of circulation results in pain, numbness, or tingling–potentially through the entire lower extremity
- Especially perilous for workers with circulatory and neuropathy issues

G.1.5.3 Neck

- Continual twist can also force subtle but constant twist at the neck as the head is twisted to view an off-center monitor

WASTEBASKET
FYTR WEAPONS

**KNOWN TO BE
HIGHLY EFFECTIVE
FOR
REDUCING PAIN & INJURY**

FYTR Rating Scale

Pain Reduction from wastebasket reposition and clutter organization: **High**
Fytr Rating Scale: **High**
Recovery Index: **High**

SELECTED FYTR WEAPONS TO CONQUER THE BYTR WASTEBASKET

SECTION GG.1

No equipment is required to turn the wastebasket or other underdesk clutter into a Friendly Device. It is an easy matter of cleaning and reorganizing the under-desk footwell allowing freedom of movement of the legs and feet. The wastebasket or any other under-desk resident should have no preference on its location.

A typical under-desk situation, compromising body-neutral position by clutter from lack of organization or attention– under-desk pencil drawer remains in place precluding under-desk keyboard tray installation, further compounding solution to user posturing

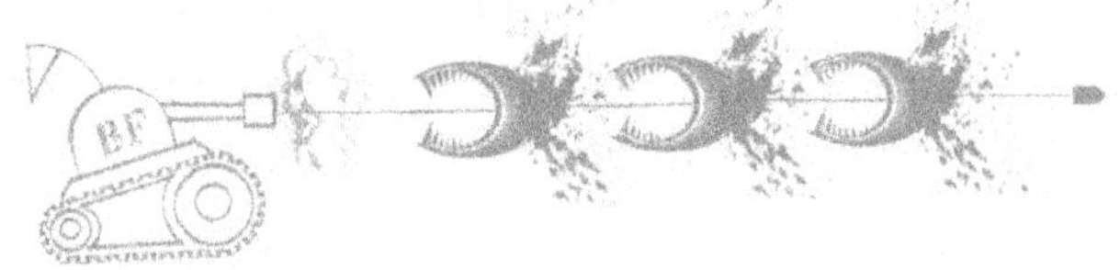
BF

DESKTOP TOOL PAIN GENERATION

BYTR PAIN DEVICE #8

SECTION H

User Danger Level Rating

BYTR Pain Generation Potential: **High**
FYTR Alert Level: **High**
Recovery Potential Index: **Medium to High**

BYTR DESKTOP TOOLS

SECTION II

Historically manually operated desktop tools are thought to be harmless and regarded as ordinary objects of everyday use, lacking concern for anything other than their intended function. Manufacturers provide little thought or design to solve potential injuries from those using these tools.

Many workers continually use these mundane tools without conscious attention to pain generation and assign it to other BYTR Devices such as the keyboard or mouse.

Each desktop device impacts hands, arms, fingers, arms, and occasionally shoulders at some level. Each device has individual characteristic pain triggers.

During each FYTR analysis, users should analyze each device to determine exact causal relationships of pain triggers.

Off-the-shelf solutions are readily available and when applied with forethought to the correct application, will successfully address injury and biomechanical issues. Some applications may require custom fabrication for unique configurations.

BYTR DESKTOP TOOL BYTR FACTS

SECTION II.1

- Many desktop tools are significant pain generators in combination with the keyboard and mouse
- Some desktop tools are the unbeknownst primary and only cause of pain irrespective of other BYTR Devices
- Effective off-the-shelf solutions *are* available, requiring detailed forethought for specific purpose application
- Alternative methods can also be practical solutions, however, these are not always obvious
- Occasionally required are custom FYTR Weapon fabrication to address symptomologies which off-the-shelf devices cannot correct
- Applying a full range of FYTR Weapons with other device corrections (keyboard, mouse, etc.), will ensure a faster user recovery ensuring an overall successful project

BYTR DESKTOP TOOL PAIN SPECIFICS

INJURIES & SYMPTOMOLOGIES

SECTION H.1.2

H.2.1 Primary Targets of Pain & Injury

- Fingers
- Hands
- Forearms

BYTR DESKTOP TOOL SPECIFICS

SECTION H.1.3

H.3.1 Secondary Targets of Pain & Injury

- Back
- Shoulder

H.3.2 Destructive Capability

- High trigger levels
- Muscle strain
- Impact trauma
- Tendinitis
- Tenosynovitis

H.3.3 Symptomology

- Cramps
- Pain/Ache
- Numbness
- Tingling (sparks)

H.3.4 Symptomology levels

- Constant to severe (debilitating)

BYTR DESKTOP TOOL

PAIN DEVELOPMENT

INJURIES & SYMPTOMOLOGIES

SECTION H.1.4

Primary Areas

H.4.1 Fingers

- Repeated forceful flexion / squeezing (staple remover, tight grip on pens, pencils, stylus)
- Repeated impacts to finger pad areas

H.4.2 Hands

- Forceful tight grip between thumb and fingers when squeezing or grasping
- Static loading during document handling/separating–repeated stress during adverse rubber banding activities
- Impact trauma when using the hand as a hammer (stapling on the desktop)

H.4.3 Forearms

- Associated adverse static and dynamic muscular activity from repetitive hand and finger action (grasping or holding)

SECTION H.5

Secondary Areas

H.5.1 Backs/Shoulders

- Forward lean and extended reach when using office tools on a desktop can exacerbate existing/developing injuries

DESKTOP TOOL

FYTR WEAPONS

CASE STUDIES

SECTION HH

HIGHLY EFFECTIVE FOR REDUCING BYTR PAIN & INJURY

The following are non-fiction, real-life actual case studies from the FYTR Files

FYTR Rating

Pain Reduction from Innocuous Tool Use: **High**
Fytr Rating Scale: **High**
Recovery Index: **High**

Case Studies
Solving Desktop Tool Pain

Virtually unrecognized, BYTR injury producing tools are found in all office workstations.

The FYTR Brigade has seen severe pain in hands, wrists, and arms of hundreds of office workers from continued use of such pain triggering tools.

Commonly ubiquitous, since the overriding parameter is low cost featuring low-quality or poor product design with little or no thought for user safety. Virtually all inexpensive desktop tools can adversely affect user anatomy when used frequently.

Below are examples from the FYTR Brigade case files of workers pointing to areas of significant pain and the specific pain triggering BYTR tools. Also presented are the FYTR Weapons used to reduce the pain.

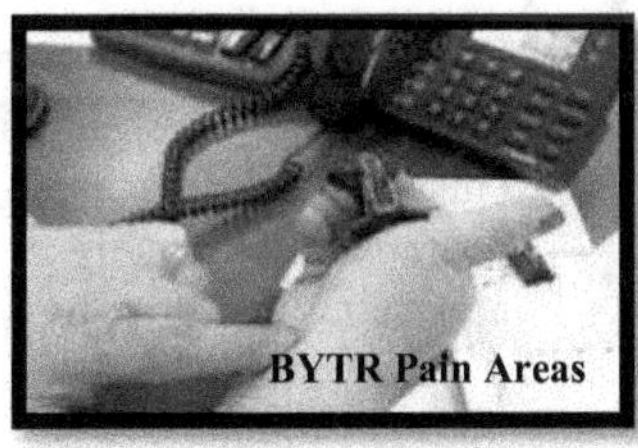

Carpal Tunnel Syndrome from using pinch type staple remover (held in hand)

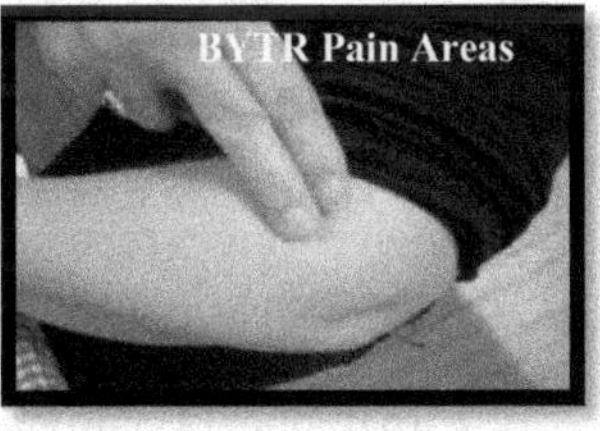

Lateral epicondylitis-lots of pain at the elbow and down through the top of the forearm

3 Hole Puncher

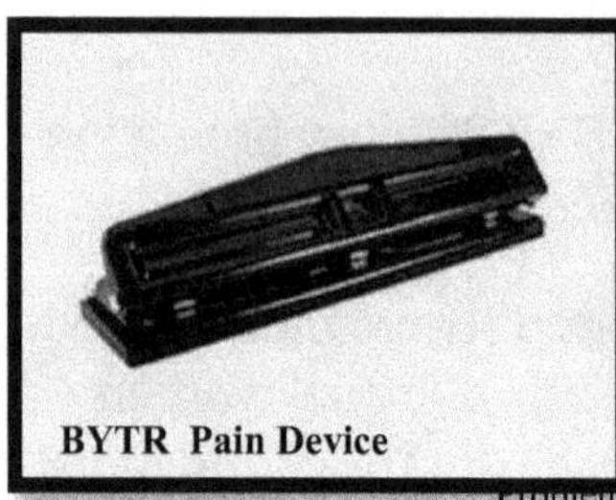

The cheap type-requiring a lot of force to press down (often used in one-handed squeeze or with elbow up)-causes overloading/injury to hand & wrist musculature (~$5)

An electric model punches 12 sheets at a time (2 & 3 holes) with no effort, making it much easier and faster saving the hands and wrists (~$75)

Staple Remover

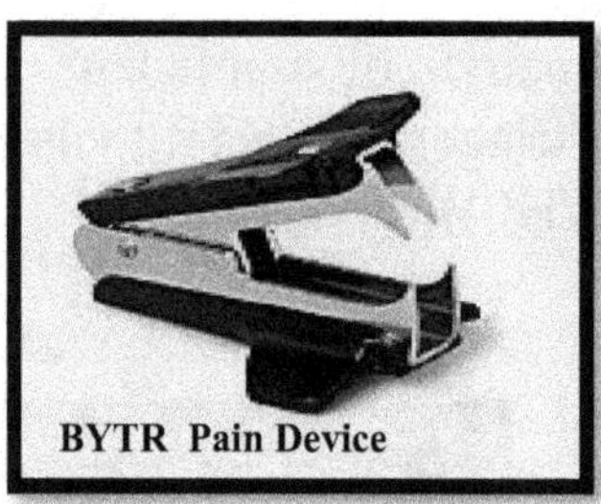

The typical cheap staple remover forces repetitive severe pinch grip making it a significant contributor to carpal tunnel syndrome, tendinitis, and tenosynovitis (~$2)

This Rubbermaid staple remover completely eliminates any grip, by easily sliding and removing staples cleanly- the **BEST** staple remover on earth, bar none! (~$15)

Hand Stapler & Electric Stapler

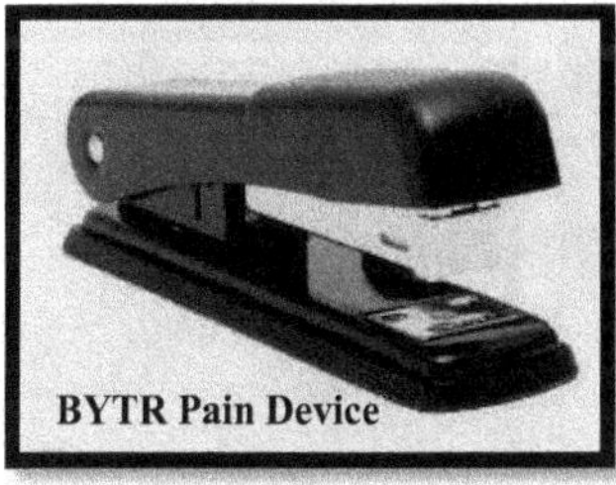
BYTR Pain Device

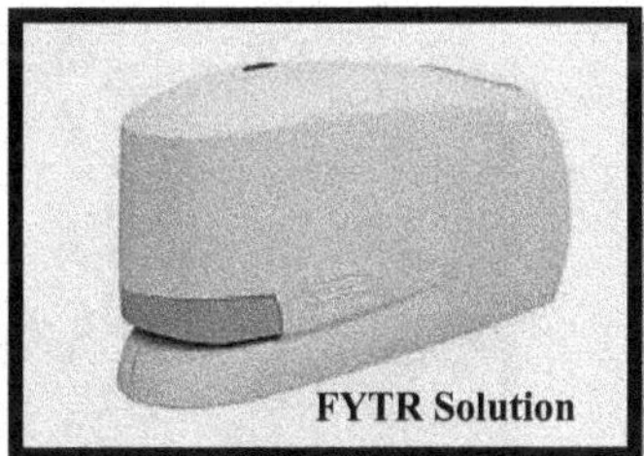
FYTR Solution

Typical cheap, standard issue stapler use requires extended reach and raised elbow in most cases, directly and *adversely* affects the wrist, forearm, and shoulder structures-especially with freestyle holding and power gripping (~$5)

An Electric stapler eliminates any adverse hand, wrist and arm action-productivity increases by eliminating stapler handling (~$35)

Pens Requiring Excessive Tight Grip

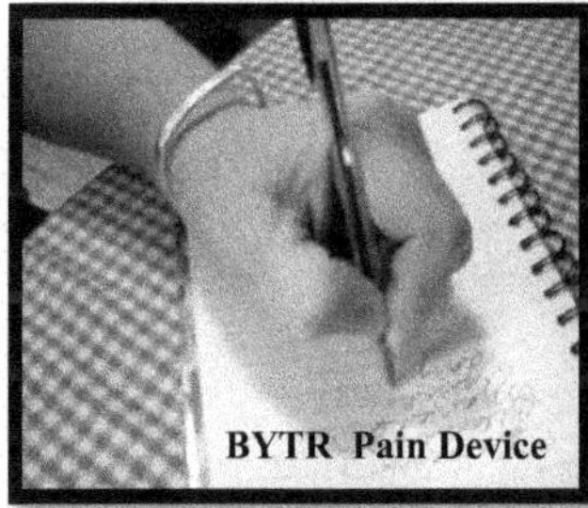
BYTR Pain Device

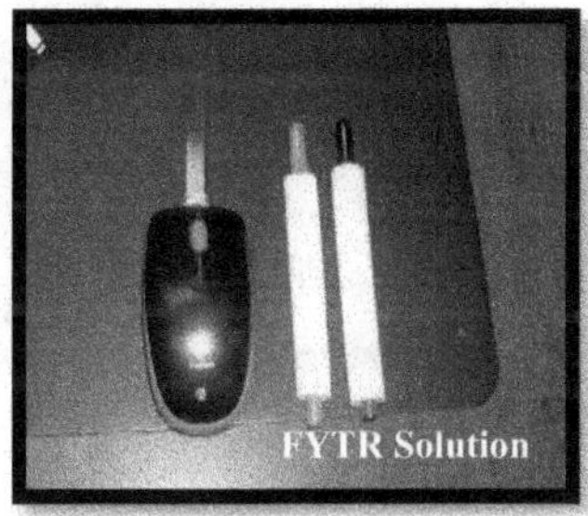
FYTR Solution

Death grip on ordinary pens contributes to CTS, tendinitis and other painful injuries-stressing everything in the hand, wrist & fingers

Foam covered pens eliminate severe pinch grip-custom diameter for different hand problems, hand size, and grip strength-used with felt-tip pens preventing too much downward force ($8)

Sort all & Custom Sorting Rack

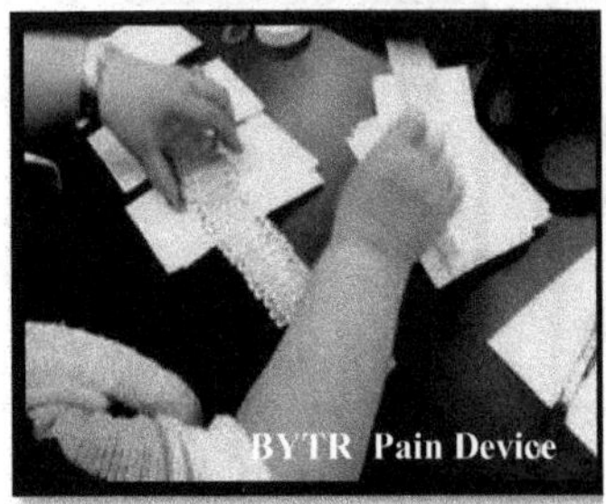
BYTR Pain Device

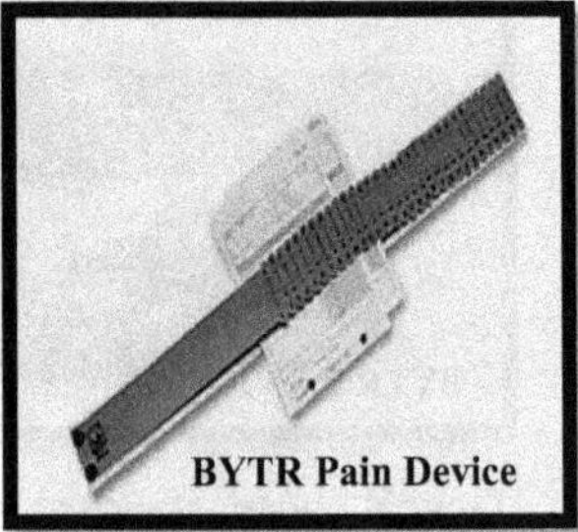
BYTR Pain Device

Continually picking up the sorting dividers with a left-handed two finger power pinch grip stresses the forearm flexor musculature, also contributing to carpal tunnel syndrome
(~$35)

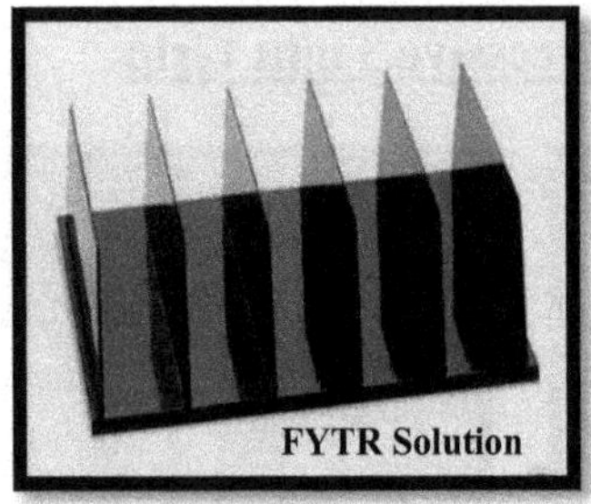
FYTR Solution

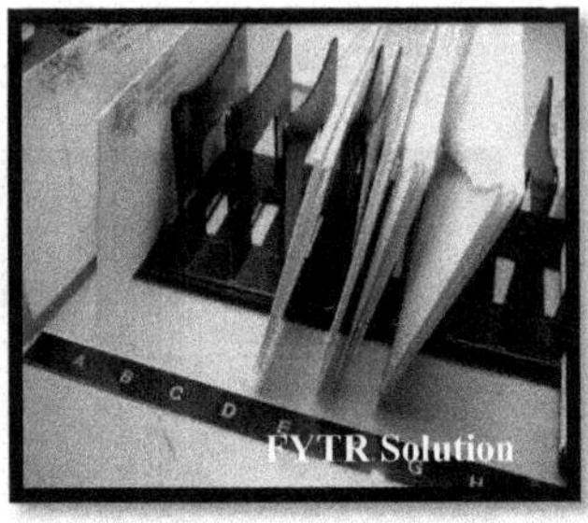

FYTR Solution

Replace the sorter by lining up small upright file organizers, labeling slots with an alphabetizing rack and easily dropping in documents- eliminates left-hand pinch grip and CTS stressors–much easier and faster to remove sorted document batches–significant productivity improvements
(~$15)
!

Rubber Banding

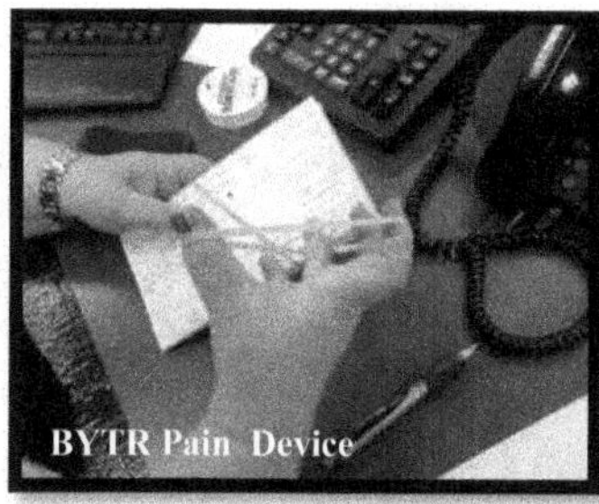

Continually stretching rubber bands as shown, strains forearm extensors and small hand musculature

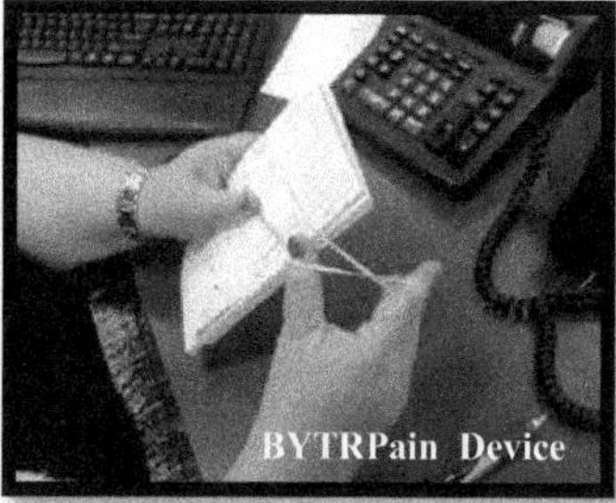

Stretching and doubling up the rubber bands continually damages hands and wrists, especially for CTS. Using one hand to hold the papers, forces a problematic and injury prone single hand stretch

Provide the correct size rubber band for the task-it's not a one size fits all scenario–the right size requires less stretching and fewer problems for hands, eliminating the doubling up ($3 per size package)

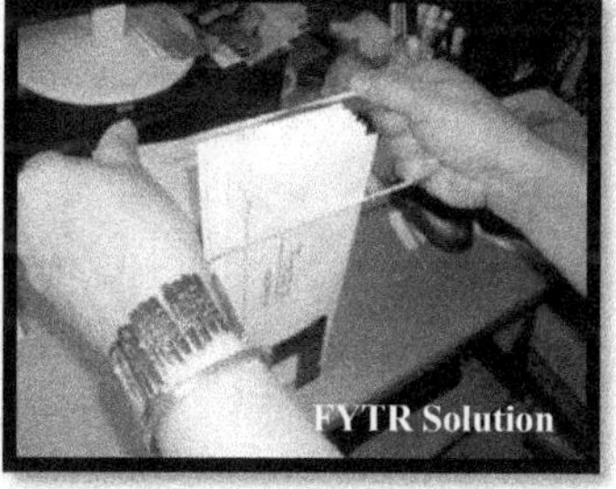

To band a group of paper items, place the batch in the alphabetizing holder-allowing two hands on the rubber band instead of one as shown above

Pulling 3-Ring Binders from Shelves

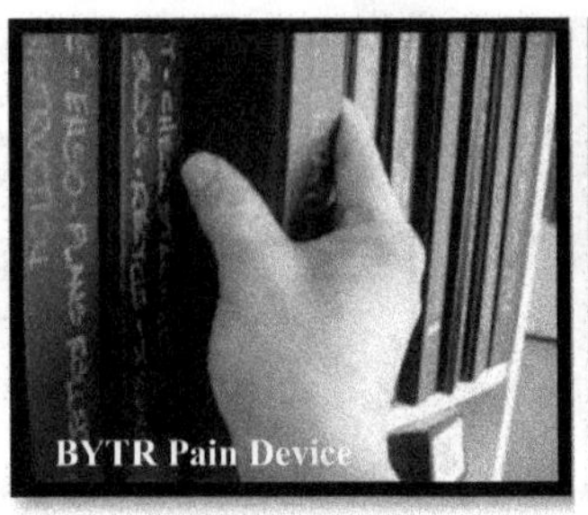
BYTR Pain Device

FYTR Solution

Pulling heavy 3 ring binders off shelving requires a power pinch grip, extended reach contributing to CTS, and arm/shoulder tendinitis

Catalog holders for the 3 ring material reduce any extended reaching (to the shelf) and excessive force on hands, wrist, and arms–information is more accessible improving productivity (~$40)

Neck Clamping a Typical Phone Handset

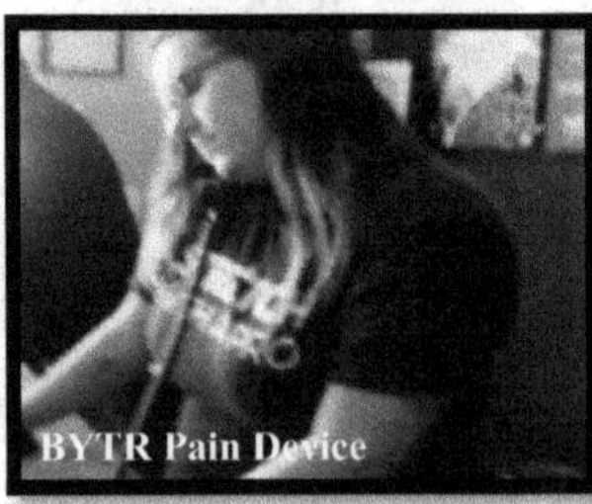
BYTR Pain Device

FYTR Solution

Clamping these handsets continually pulls neck musculature on one side and stretches opposite side resulting in muscle strain, neural and vasculature compression with resultant pain and numbness

A good headset (corded or cordless) completely offloads any head, neck and upper back strain–also increases productivity as handset handling is eliminated (Hellodirect.com ~$15)

Section III

Addendum

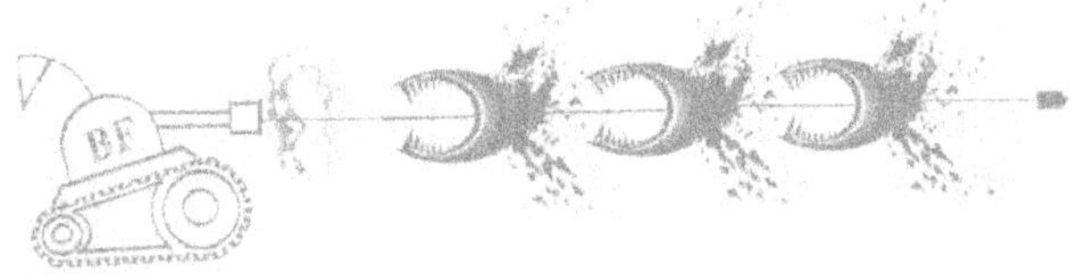
BF

SUCCESS STORIES FROM

THE FREQUENT FYTR CASE FILES

ACTUAL FYTR DEVICE DEPLOYMENT

ACTUAL FYTR DEVICE SUCCESS STORIES

Pain enough to threaten jobs and careers.

Here are two actual projects, about two people in enough pain to diminish their ability to perform professional job tasks.

The first, Ellie Bea, works for a large municipality. An environmental engineer, she analyzes and documents scientific data. She "loves her job" and wanted to do everything possible to keep it.

The second, Tommie Joe is a person of high intellect, a Ph.D. from Stanford and a Post Doctorate from Harvard. With such credentials, he documents his work in scientific journals and writes seriously long grant proposals, spending a large part of his workday on a keyboard.

Both suffered high-level pain, and both needed help to lessen their pain to continue with their careers.

Both are extensive keyboard jockeys. Both tried different things unsuccessfully. Both knew Ergonomics was the right direction but were unaware of the right path.

From a cursory viewpoint, these cases appeared as typical office ergonomics. In actuality, like many, both were complex but very, very subtle.

The Case of Ellie Bea

This began with an inquiring eye-opening email, finding our website through research and desperation.

Email #1 from Ellie Bea (verbatim)

> *"I have been battling my employer (or really their lack of much assistance) for almost the entire last year regarding a problem I have had with mostly my right wrist (but also my left wrist and both arms at times). I have a work comp lawsuit just about at settlement–but there is one serious problem:*
>
> *"I have not been able to get the problem corrected! I have had numerous doctor and physical therapy visits. <u>My employer finally got me an ergonomic assessment from an outside company, but the assessor, an occupational therapist basically told me I looked fine.</u> I requested an ergo keyboard, which did help substantially with some of the problems. But I still have chronic, immediate pain from using my mouse. I don't know what to do and I can't find anyone who truly knows what they're doing as far as setting up a desk/mouse so I do not have perpetual pain. Do you know of anyone you can recommend that is in (my state)? Any help would be very appreciated.*
>
> *"Thanks"*

Like many typical power keyboard users, her symptomology began as an innocuous irritation and progressing to current levels of high-level pain and debilitation.

During our discussions, she revealed details of an assessment by an Occupational Therapist who took only 15 minutes, did nothing and cost the company $700. WOW! $700 for improving nothing and for only a 15-minute analysis? Unbelievable!

The question is: why couldn't this Occupational Therapist who performed the original analysis really do anything meaningful? An obvious answer. Not only did he not do anything, but he also didn't even show any real great concern for Ellie Bea, and for that, he cannot be forgiven.

The result: Ellie Bea *He abandoned Ellie Bea and left her in pain.* Why was management so resistant to providing her real help? Did they not care about her? I believe it was not intentional, but merely wanting to resolve the situation as painlessly as possible (through inaction). This appears tantamount to ignoring the circumstances, hoping the problem will go away on its own.

Remember, you cannot see this type of pain and it is sometimes dismissed as fictional. It is, however, very complex and very, very subtle.

After some conversation, she replied, offering some history.

Email #2 from Ellie Bea (verbatim)

> *"After starting to develop a nearly constant discomfort in my right wrist, I did minimal internet research and found the vertical mouse. I asked my boss for this and received it in early summer 2013. This was the set up I had last fall, through the period when I was receiving PT, and perhaps or perhaps not coincidentally, through the time that I was in the most overall pain throughout this ordeal.*
>
> *"Through the months of PT, nothing was changing; in fact, I sometimes felt more/different pain than I had felt before. Not getting any better and getting frustrated by the constant pain I was working through, I requested and received the natural keyboard. Within just a few weeks of receiving this keyboard, most of the pain I had experienced in my left wrist/arm/elbow was gone and there were modest improvements in my right, particularly, the burning in my elbow mostly went away. I think this keyboard allowed my wrists to be in a straight line with my arms instead of kinked. Also, I think the center tenting of the keyboard, wrist rest, and downward slope toward the back of the keyboard helped things. The only thing that I didn't like about this keyboard is how large it was on the right and that I felt like my arm reaches out really far to reach the mouse."*

Another round of communication and then this from Ellie Bea.

Email #3 from Ellie Bea (verbatim)

"Hi Ian

"Thanks for checking. I have gotten disgustingly little movement from my employer or from the pending lawsuit. My lawyer put in a settlement several weeks ago and I haven't heard anything yet. I asked in the settlement to have a trained, certified professional ergonomic specialist. I also tried following up with the OT that did the previous ergonomic assessment, but he just told me he was only contracted to do a one-time assessment and that was it (and I wonder what the heck the assessment was even for, then).

"I just continue trial-and-erroring (on my own) to figure out an arrangement that doesn't hurt. After talking with you, I got rid of my vertical mouse and tried the standard mouse. That actually gave me more pain. Now I am re-trying a chair with arm support, trying to rest my arm on that and hang my hand off the edge and use my touchpad which is laying on my desk. No big difference so far with anything."

Ellie Bea was trying everything; after all, her job and career were 'on the line' and at-risk.

1. B4–Original keyboard

2. B4–Reverting to the original mouse

3. B4–Microsoft Natural KB with Evoluent mouse

I couldn't just stand idly by while someone was in pain. Ellie Bea stated she could not afford any payment, I offered to help her as best I could for the munificent price of a Starbucks gift card.

She agreed to follow explicit instructions. I requested she enlist a pal to take close-up photographs of her hands, workstation, back, shoulder and other impacting factors. I also sent specific charts and body maps with instructions on reporting and analysis. I got back 30 pages of data and photos. Ellie Bea did her homework.

Next, we spent a couple hours on the phone going over her case with notes, and data in front of me.

After assessing her ongoing pain, we crafted a work plan including a list of specific equipment which she immediately bought and installed, and with guidance, began using it properly.

Her symptomology immediately went down, way down.

4. New–Kinesis Freestyle KB and Kensington TB

5. New–Getting used to the Kensington TB

Email #4 from Ellie Bea (verbatim)

"Ian: Following up quickly -

"The changes that were made at your recommendation have allowed me to partake in my normal life again. *For the last several months, I couldn't enjoy my hobbies such as gardening or bicycling; I was in too much pain and fearful I would further aggravate my painful condition. While the pain isn't completely gone from my right wrist, it's substantially diminished. I am in relatively minor pain in my right wrist only when I am using my keyboard heavily at work, and the pain is almost completely gone from my arm and elbow. Even when I am keyboarding heavily enough to elicit pain, I can manage to work through the pain, and more importantly, I can enjoy myself outside of work. Thanks for helping me and I look forward to continuing to work with you so we can hopefully troubleshoot and take care of the rest of the right wrist pain.*

"Thanks again!!"

A Starbucks gift card arrived in the mail with a warm handwritten note on a Hallmark greeting card.

It made me smile

Here is a summary of Ellie Bea's project specifics.

Medical Conditions/Symptomology *(Ellie Bea)*

Left Arm

- Mild to moderate pain in the last 6 months

Right Arm

- Moderate to significant pain & burning on medial and lateral elbow epicondyles (AKA tennis elbow & golfers elbow)
- Burning pain through the dorsal and ventral (top & bottom) forearms
- Constant pain, soreness, and fatigue throughout entire wrist structure

Previous Mods Trialed/Results *(Ellie Bea)*

- Microsoft Natural keyboard installed with a reduction in left and right arm symptomology
- Evoluent vertical mouse installed increasing pain prompting a return to the standard mouse

New Modifications Installed Per Instructions/Results *(Ellie Bea)*

- Kinesis Freestyle split keyboard- reduction in right and left arm pain
- Kensington Trackball Pro on right side- further reducing right wrist symptomology
- Kensington Trackball Pro trialed on left side further reducing right wrist symptomology with a new mild triggering on left side
- Super-secret input device for other mouse functions-further reducing wrist pain

At last check, Ellie Bea was still working at the job "she just loves," and in decidedly less pain. She confessed of a minor setback in helping her husband clean their lawnmower using an air nozzle. Some pain flared up but after some rest, she recuperated. She admitted knowing better, but "sacrificed" herself for her sweetheart.

I teased her.

AUTHORS note

I came away from this project with a great sense of satisfaction and gratification, especially knowing I had a positive impact on Ellie Bea's future.

The Case of Tommy Joe

Tommy Joe's arm symptomology was as equally severe as Ellie Bea's; steadily increasing, becoming more and more troublesome in his professional day, and impacting his ability to keyboard. He (like many computer jockeys) became concerned if this was the beginning of the end.

Tommy Joe worried whether the diminishing keyboarding capability would impact his career. As an expert in a prominent field, he requires the ability to keyboard.

After analysis and the initial modifications installed, he revealed his symptomology initially significantly decreased. However, after several months, he noticed it settled down but still hadn't entirely disappeared. I eventually recommended an additional modification for his workstation.

It was a Contour RollerMouse. We sat over coffee and familiarized him with the Roller's characteristics. The one observation he so astutely made was that it makes SO MUCH sense to bring hand input (i.e. mousing) to the middle. The Roller eliminates the outward arm rotation, which is a known contributor to right arm symptomology.

These photos show his old workstation and new modifications.

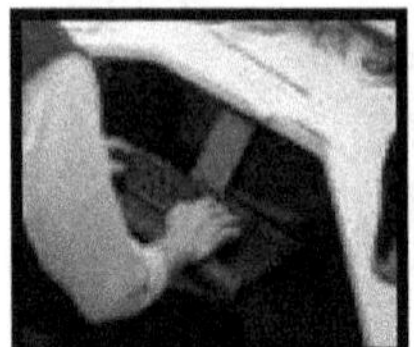
Old workstation triggering elbow (lateral epicondyle) & forearm pain

Previous touchpad forcing static loading on fingers, flexors and extensor forearm musculature

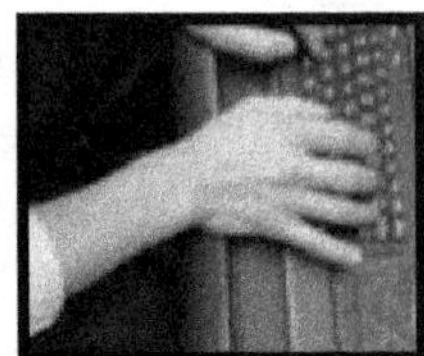
Bad ulnar deviation (hand turned outward from the midline of the forearm)

Less inward rotation & ulnar deviation with a split keyboard having less stress on the forearm and elbow structures

Using the thumb to roll mouse leaving hands in home row position reducing loading on forearms

Right-hand thumb rolling with the Kensington trackball still used on the desktop for a change of pace.

At last report, Tommy Joe continues using the RollerMouse and is incrementally improving.

But like Ellie Bea, he had a minor setback. It seems his energetic high school aged son challenged him to a push-up contest. Well, Dad took up the challenge (what Dad wouldn't?), and his right elbow let him know he shouldn't have. Like Ellie Bea, a recreational injury had exacerbated the occupational injury.

So what? They're both injuries, and when care is not taken, personal or recreational activities can make any occupational injury worse.

The overriding thought for both Tommy Joe and Ellie Bea here is: an injury, is an injury, **is an injury** and you must let it heal, **not** subject it to additional strain when away from the workstation (such as using your husband's air tool or challenging your son.)

It doesn't matter where or how it happened, whether recreational or occupational, your body doesn't care. Many have the mistaken notion that just because they are away from the keyboard or mouse, the hurt won't occur. They couldn't be more wrong.

Both Ellie Bea and Tommy Joe *probably* knew better, a fact, both admit. Tommy Joe succumbed to social pressure and in case you are interested, Dad out pushed-up son two to one.

Here is a summary of Tommy Joe's project specifics.

Medical Conditions/Symptomology *(Tommy Joe)*

- Moderate to significant pain at the outside right elbow (lateral epicondyle)
- Moderate to significant pain on the dorsal (top) of right forearm

Previous Mods Trialed/Results *(Tommy Joe)*
Installation of the keyboard with built-in touchpad device on a keyboard (right side) without position change capability did not address his symptomology.

New Modifications Installed Per Our Instructions/Results *(Tommy Joe)*

- Kinesis Freestyle split keyboard- right arm pain reduction
- Kensington Trackball on right side-further reducing right arm symptomology
- Contour RollerMouse installed, further reducing right arm lateral epicondyle pain eliminating outward rotation to reach the Kensington Trackball
- Kensington Trackball moved to left side, completely removing all outward right-hand rotation allowing right elbow to recover and to keep habitual usage of a known input device (Kensington)

REASONS EQUIPMENT FAILED
(For Ellie Bea)

Ellie Bea's Evoluent Brand Mouse

In concept, it sounds and looks great. It orients the hand in a vertical position, just like you would naturally shake hands with someone. If it works in pain reduction, it is successful and by all means, should remain in place.

However, it just wasn't the right fit and application for Ellie Bea.

Experience shows some folks swear by them, and that's just *delightful*! You can't argue with success and if you perceive a benefit from the Evoluent (or any other device), then, by all means, continue using it and ***don't let any hotshot Ergonomist tell you otherwise***. If it works, reducing your pain, it then becomes Ergonomics at its finest.

I think the Evoluent is something everyone should at least try. Like any device, you don't know if it'll work until trialed-just don't keep it around if it doesn't. Like Ellie Bea or any good Ergonomist, keep trying other things until you (emulating Sherlock Holmes) come to a workable conclusion based on objective thinking and analysis.

Ellie Bea made an in-depth evaluation of The Evoluent, using it in battle conditions for an extended period. She determined it did not do what she needed. It did not fix her pain. Nothing wrong with that, it's like a size 8 foot and a size 6 Nike shoe. Both are perfect, but it is just not a fit. A device more specific to Ellie Bea's biomechanical issues was called for.

The same can be said for any computer device, no matter the brand, model, or application.

Ellie Bea's Microsoft Natural Keyboard.

The unique shape of the Natural has been documented as beneficial for millions of users and is overall a creative design. However, like the scenario with the Evoluent, the Natural just didn't quite do everything needed for successfully addressing Ellie Bea's biomechanics with the tented shape only being partially beneficial. I know of people who swear by them, but like the Evoluent, it just didn't do everything Ellie Bea needed (Nike shoe size and foot size principle).

Ellie Bea's Standard Mouse

The standard mouse has been around for what seems forever and still used by millions without incident. But like any other input device, if the user is prone to developing, or already has symptomology, the standard mouse can sometimes be a deal-breaker for career continuation or advancement.

Here are a couple other problems with the standard mouse usage:

(1.) The first problem is not the fault of the mouse itself, but rather its location; usually on the desktop, forcing extended reach affecting shoulders, elbows and mostly forearms musculature.

The result? Significant pain flares in these areas, especially at the "tennis elbow" (lateral epicondyle) site.

(2.) Second is how many hold the mouse, unconsciously acting as if it is actually a live mouse and using a death grip, squeeze it tightly. Nothing wrong with holding onto something of value like this, however, this death grip squeeze results in constant static loading on the hand, wrist, or forearm structures which fatigue over time with resultant pain. The mouse doesn't mind, but your body surely will.

(3.) Finally, the actual mouse use or movement is another issue. In combination with the death grip, many anchor the forearm and wrist on the desktop or chair armrest, pivoting the hand at the wrist moving the mouse side to side, in an arc. Called ulnar and radial deviation it moves the hand midline away from the arm midline, to the left or right direction of the ulnar or radius arm bones (waving goodbye).

This continual pivot point wrist motion is highly injurious repeatedly stretching and bending tendons, tendon sheaths, and the median nerve through the carpal tunnel. Too much of this left and right movement and carpal tunnel syndrome (CTS) shows up.

With forearms locked on the desktop or chair armrest, front-to-back mouse movement requires repeated finger flexion and extension. This action is yet another action affecting forearm musculature and associated tendons passing through the carpal tunnel contributing to CTS.

Standard mouse usage with these movements is highly contributory to a vast majority of computer user hand, wrist and forearm problems we see.

REASONS EQUIPMENT FAILED
(For Tommy Joe)

Tommy Joe's Touchpad Mouse.

Full disclosure, touchpads are great for some applications, just not for Tommy Joe. Yes, I've installed them from time to time under certain circumstances, and they work great for those who have severe arm movement issues. Touchpads minimize extended reach and outward rotation when placed at or near the keyboard centerline..

Other successful applications for users having a specific hand or arm problem, includes using larger graphics pads having a pen type stylus for input and cursor control.

Unfortunately, touchpads exist on a vast majority of all laptops and is associated with triggering repetitive motion injuries such as tenosynovitis, tendinitis or CTS. For the average keyboardist with developing or having a predisposition to a RMI, the touchpad becomes a pain triggering BYTR Device.

The touchpads in Tommy Joe's previous workstation require a static loaded finger posture to press down and move on the touchpad surface for cursor control. This static loading (affecting hand and wrist structures) is a primary reason touchpad power users report an associated significant level of pain. Don't believe me? Ask a veteran power laptop user their opinion.

Touchpad Tidbits

Before large-scale touchpad use, some past generation keyboards featured a mini trackball placed at the keyboard centerline just below the spacebar, available for use by both hands. Other trackball laptop models had a small trackball on the lower right-hand corner. Some were glossy and smooth, and body oils or sweat, made them difficult to control. The solution involved sanding down the slick surface to a matte finish providing more friction between fingers and ball. Unlike the touchpad, these on-board trackballs reduced arm movement and eliminated hand grip and static finger positioning. The Contour system follows this philosophy nicely.

REASONS THIS EQUIPMENT WORKS
(For Both Ellie Bea & Tommy Joe)

Trackballs

I love trackballs, but only in specific circumstances and for specific reasons. I have installed and have also *removed* plenty over the years. Why removed, you ask? Because they were the wrong style for a specific individual and their unique biomechanical issues. Remember FYTR philosophy states *"application isn't everything, it is the only thing."*

How can a trackball be wrong for someone? Great Question!

A myriad of different trackball input device exists. Some have balls on the top, some have balls on the side, and some have balls on the front. Some balls are big, some are small, and some are medium-sized. Trackball design has advanced over the years and like many things Ergonomic, the ideal trackball is (get this) the one that functions best for **you**. *Finding* it is the challenge.

So how do you do that? Don't just blindly throw one into the fray and hope it works. That's not the way to do it! You can successfully eliminate pain by trial and continued re-evaluation with an in-depth analysis determining the causal relationship and then apply a specific trackball. That is the approach.

The right trackball must be fit to the way the individual works, with analysis on hand action and specific symptomology, will detail what to offload. Done with Tommy Joe and Ellie Bea, the final recommendation for both was one of my favorites: the Kensington Expert Mouse.

Kensington Expert Mouse Trackball

Kensington Slimblade Trackball

The Kensington places the hand, wrist, and arm aggregate into a more body-neutral posture unlike the standard mouse. Plus, the 4-button programmability replaces hitting the <esc>, <tab>, <backspace>, <enter> and combination (<alt-6>) keys with perilous hand postures called ulnar and radial deviation. Eliminating these adverse postures allows workers in pain to recover and importantly allows placing physical and intellectual energy into work tasks instead of addressing pain triggered by a poorly designed input device.

Interestingly enough both of my "charges" here moved the Kensington trackball to the left side, trying a new approach in addressing right wrist/arm pain, and both Ellie Bea and Tommy Joe enjoyed that kind of flexibility.

A good trackball, when *applied under the right condition,* can do wonders in reducing significant pain. The Kensington trackball may NOT be right for everyone, but they sure worked well for Ellie Bea and Tommy Joe.

Split Keyboards

There have been numerous attempts in keyboard redesign over the years, many now defunct from bad design, bad marketing or lack of public understanding or acceptance (sales). The Kinesis Freestyle meets many criteria for addressing forearm and elbow pain, mainly eliminating inward arm rotation, allowing hands to move away from keyboard centerline into a body-neutral position, unlike a standard one-piece keyboard.

This elimination of inward arm rotation used to reach the home row can be the difference between pain and non-pain. With pain from adverse postures reduced, muscle activation is also reduced allowing a high recovery potential allowing Ellie Bea and Tommy Joe to continue keyboarding- high benefit corollaries.

REASONS WHY THIS EQUIPMENT WORKS

Especially For Tommy Joe

Contour RollerMouse Red plus™,

Both Tommy Joe and Ellie Bea love it.

Large palm rests eliminate ventral (palmar) pressure on wrist and carpal tunnel area

The Contour RollerMouse Red plus™, like the Kinesis Contoured™ keyboard, has large palm rests allowing hands to rest on the fleshy parts of the palm (proper names are: thenar eminence and hypothenar eminence). The posture completely offloads any contact pressure from the underside of the wrist and the sensitive carpal tunnel.

The RollerMouse cursor controls, placed in the middle, (just below the spacebar) encourages using the scroll, left, and right clicks, copy and paste by the strong thumb.

I wouldn't recommend one of these for someone who has a damaged carpometacarpal joint-thumb knuckle-(who incidentally we placed a Cirque touchpad), but for someone like Tommy Joe having static loading and right arm rotation problems, it *is* perfect.

The central location of the cursor controls also eliminates any outward rotation saving extraneous arm motions for the mouse (or other input devices) usage. Correctly set up (emphasis on the *correctly*) it naturally places the entire arm in a fully relaxed, or even neutral positioning, offloading all subtle and inadvertent forearm and upper arm loading.

Right-hand finger rolling mouse control with left-hand finger-clicking action

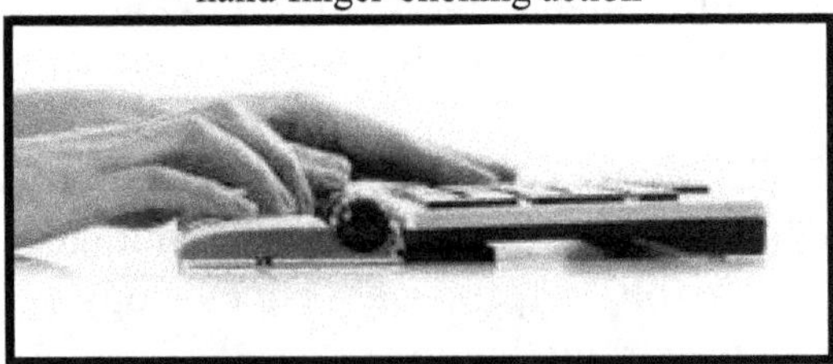

Left-hand thumb action for mouse control and Right-hand click/roller action

These benefits occur once the user becomes fluent with the new unconventional cursor control. Frequently, users develop personal quirks or touches on using the roller bar with the cursor copy and paste keys. Ergonomics at its most creative.

Understand the RollerMouse is a semi-custom application. It could benefit almost everyone and definitely addresses specific symptomology.

However, don't let anyone else sit at your workstation and use it. They'll probably give you some friendly ribbing about your "new mouse".

Also, with using the Contour's unique roller bar, there are creative ways one can move the cursor and click by using one hand (thumb) on the roller bar and the other on the inner guide shaft or the left click button(pressing the entire roller actuates a left click). This works for some since it takes a bit of dexterity to keep the cursor placed when using the thumb to roll.

Often, the cursor will move by the inadvertent action of the thumb when clicking with the roller bar. Using the roller bar with the other fingers enables more control for placement clicking. An alternative is using the non-rolling hand to click by pushing down the entire support bar or the left click button, as the roller, well, rolls on.

One little-understood characteristic of the RollerMouse is the multitude of effective ways to use it. Unlike a standard mouse or even trackball, it allows incredible flexibility for users having multiple symptomologies.

For the suitable user and appropriate application, the RollerMouse has proven to reduce hand, finger, and arm symptomology. It gets two thumbs up, not while rolling of course.

As a general rule, we have discovered that installing the RollerMouse without removing the trackball or mouse is helpful. Since the Contour takes some acclimation, keeping both has proven very effective in still allowing occasional habitual mouse usage and seamless transition. Frequently the trackball or mouse is permanently kept with the Contour for simple posture variance.

However long they split time between the RollerMouse and their old mouse/trackball, their symptomology improves by reducing the continual adverse postures, always a plus.

Eventually, after noticeable improvements and the regular mouse or trackball eliminated, many folks install a RollerMouse in their home workstation.

Bottom Line

The best news is both Ellie Bea and Tommy Joe experienced high-level pain reduction with off-the-shelf, readily available, albeit relatively unknown hardware devices.

The most crucial element of each case was proper biomechanical analysis and appropriate application of hardware to hand action observed. Mostly it was their willingness to follow logical advice, trying something new and evaluating purpose and effectiveness.

I helped these two individuals mostly because of their willingness for open communication while working through their issues.

These Office Ergonomics projects were in a different geographical state, clear across the country, and performed by remote control. It should speak to you that Ergonomics can be effectively applied this way provided the practitioner's knowledge base is deep and people skills are sharp.

This remote control Ergonomics project methodology can effectively address any computer workstation Ergonomics or industrial injury issue. Follow-up and communication are the keys. However, I am saddened there are not more Ergo types practicing in such a remote control or even with an in-depth manner like this.

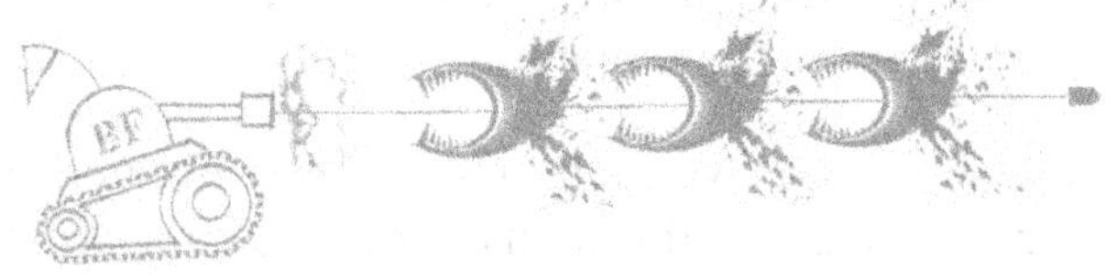

VOODOO ERGONOMICS GALLERY

OFFICE TOOLS & EQUIPMENT

Tools, equipment, and furnishings advertised or labeled as “Ergonomic” generally are ***NOT.*** These only present themselves as false declarations solely for marketing purposes. Analyze and determine truthfulness in stated descriptions before any implementation.

*AKA BYTR Pain Generating Devices

VOODOO ERGONOMICS
GALLERY

A continual nemesis of any BYTR FYTR is the multitude of things falsely claimed to be "Ergonomic."

Become cognizant of such charlatan devices. Educate yourself, your students, and your charges in the harm these "snake oil" things provide.

It is up to you, FYTR, to impart proper guidance as to valid solutions to problems encountered in computer workstations. Realize that for every legitimate device there are tenfold false and lying inventions, contraptions, or gimmicks called "Ergonomic" solely for marketing purposes attempting to fool and delude end users.

Understand that it is your duty to know these fallacies and to impart a valued knowledge of computer tasks to help users heal their pain and continue with their career unimpeded.

Study these well and add them to your repertoire of falsities strengthening your case and care.

There are those who would place profit above their fellow Human's health, making these yet another of the FYTRs real enemies.

Visit The BYTR Blog for more Voodoo Ergonomic Devices.

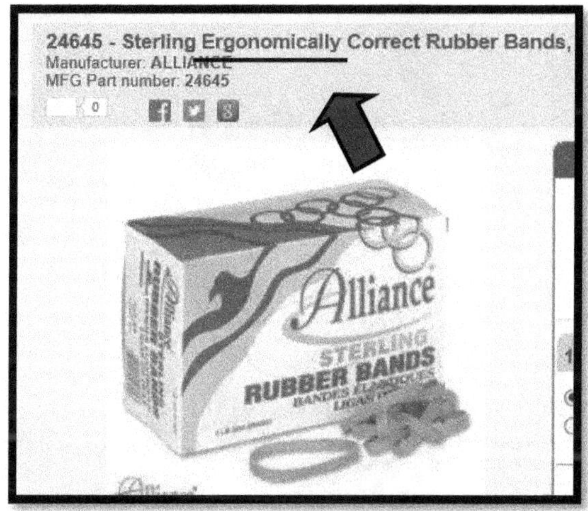

"Ergonomically Correct" Rubber Bands?

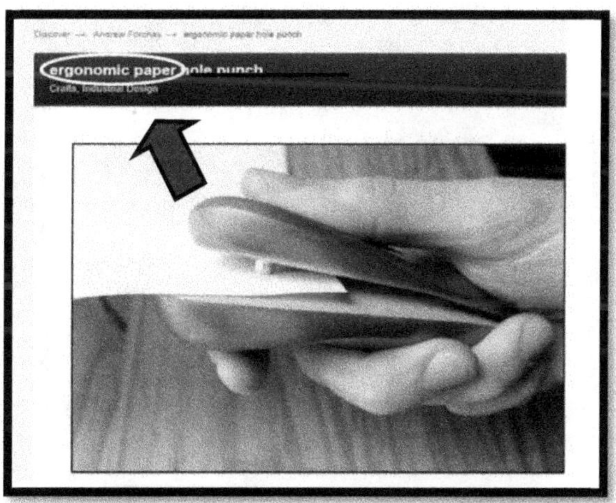

Another definitive BYTR Pain inducing device for hands and thumbs (p. 203)

Low-Fat Pringles

Potato chips are of course a classic snack and it's really e... them while typing. The problem is, they can often be greasy and messy.

Low-fat Pringles, however, solve this problem by being both ergonomically stacked for sequential eating between tweets, and are also low on grease.

The "Ergonomic" Potato Chip

Hunter Fan 56" Brushed Nickel Ergonomic Ceiling Fan

This Brushed Nickel Ergonomic fan from Hunter is a solid conte... fan, great to brig... any room. It comes with a remote to make using ... breeze. T... moves air quietly and so efficiently in fact it is backed by Hunter'... lifetime warranty. Hunter Ceiling Fans have been energy

The "Ergonomic" Ceiling Fan for "Ergonomic" ceilings

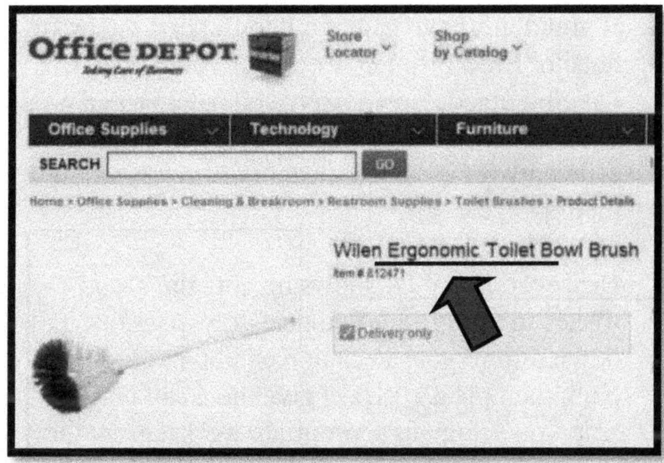

For "Ergonomic" Toilet Bowls

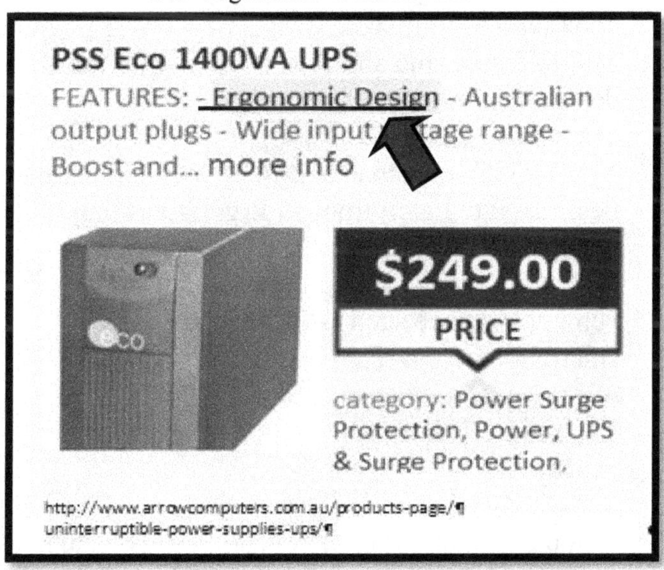

The Never Handled "Ergonomic" UPS

Final End Note

If you don't have pain, you don't need me or any hotshot Ergo Pro. I don't care if you work hanging upside down from a chandelier in a pitch black room. If you are productive, and can efficiently crank out a meaningful work product then good for you.

However, if BYTR shows up, and the blood rushes to your head, you get dizzy, pass out, fall down, injure your neck and end up in chronic pain, then please, please give me a call and I'll help you set up an appropriate workstation. Or you can enlist the aid of a known BYTR FYTR. Perhaps you might even educate yourself (this book) and become your own BYTR FYTR, Your health, career, and ability to support your family depends on it.

You MUST learn to take care of yourself, learn to be proactive. Learn from an Ergo Pro as they perform an assessment. Caring for yourself is highly important as long as you are using any computer device such as PC, laptops, tablets, smartphones, and iPads.

Ergonomics should be looked upon as serious healthcare.

If you don't take care of yourself, or instigate help from a real FYTR then at least watch out! ***BYTR (or DYVR) will find you!***

Dear BYTR FYTR

By completing the lessons in this manual, you have furthered your awareness and training towards assembling your knowledge of Ergonomics and how to fight the BYTRS. By correctly applying the knowledge contained herein, you have joined the ranks of the BYTR FYTR BRIGADE.

Email me how you got on with this manual and how you have successfully fought the BYTRS. You can reach me through the contact link on our web.

www.ergoinc.com.

If you have found this manual useful or inspirational, I would welcome a review on sites like Amazon, Barnes & Noble, Goodreads, BookLikes, etc.

Email me the link to your review, your name & address and I'll send you a BYTR FYTR badge for each review along with a personalized BYTR FYTR Certificate with a gold seal, suitable for framing allowing you to show the world your accomplishment (p.310).

Graphic by Chloë L. Barson

Beware The BYTR

BYTR FYTR Certificate

Acknowledgements

Besides those respectably listed in the front page dedications, I gratefully acknowledge the following folks who have provided insight, critique, friendship, inspiration and company in my pursuit of completing yet another Ergonomic Adventure. Without their help and friendship, I honestly would not have been able to hit the finish line. My sincerest thanks go to them and my apologies to those inadvertently left out. However, you know who you are and undoubtedly will never cease to give me grief reminding me of this oversight.

I offer my thanks, raise a glass and give a tip o' the hat to these folks for their wonderful contributions and/or inspirations, listed in no particular order: Erwin T., Philip Michael, Mac-in-on, Andy I., Rough Tough, The Susan, Jeffie, Scotty, Cracker, Joy S., Wayne M., Steve Mo., Gordonzo, Pace, Hannah S., Peter B, Alison HO., Karen W., Jon B, Loren A., Tom R., KJ, Sailer, Lance P., Hector, Wilson and the many (unfortunately too numerous to name) Voc, CM, HR, Safety, Ergo & Other Pros I know who have also made contributions.

And of course to those staunch supporters in my Writing Club, especially: Michele C., Kris G., Ed S., Spike, Kathy McM., Linda A., Ben, Carla, Ashleigh B., among others.

Other Books by the Author

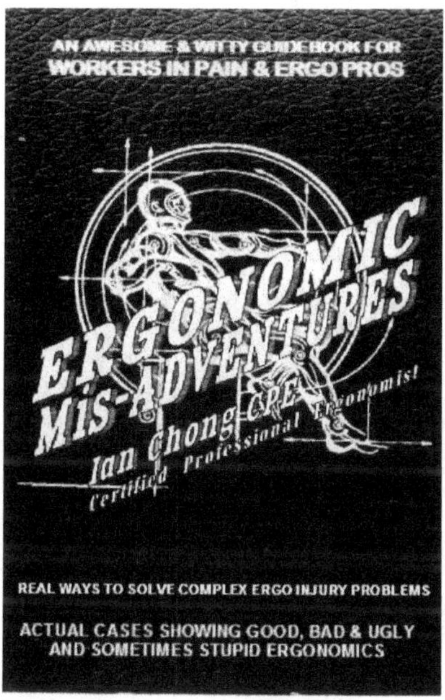

Ergonomic Mis-Adventures

An AWESOME and witty guidebook for workers in pain and Ergo pros of any level. Geared to enlighten and inspire both. No boring textbook, No big words. No scientific jargon. Just entertaining adventures and stories showing real applications of REAL ERGONOMICS, also exposing its "DARK or SAD SIDE". Amusing and informative by showing successful case studies, it includes concepts and examples illustrating how to take control of (your) work-related pain, fix it and get on with your life. GOOD, BAD & UGLY AND SOMETIMES STUPID ERGONOMICS REVEALED!!! A tear-out sheet with Professional Super Secrets and methods for you to help control your occupational injury. If you have work-related pain or want to help someone who does, you'll enjoy the adventure.–Available on Amazon.com

Other Books by the Author

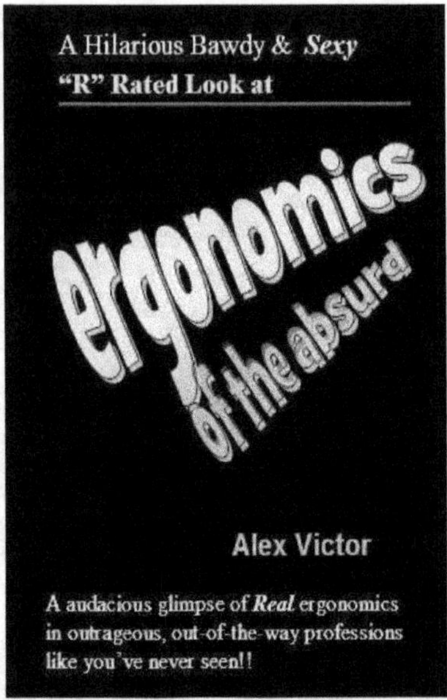

A Hilarious Bawdy & Sexy
"R" Rated Look at
ergonomics
of the absurd
Alex Victor
A audacious glimpse of Real ergonomics
in outrageous, out-of-the-way professions
like you've never seen!!

Ergonomics of the Absurd (almost "R" rated)

A never before revealed hilarious, laugh-out-loud, somewhat bawdy look at the heretofore serious world of Ergonomics It's an in-depth look at audacious, out-of-the-way professions and their dangers of occupational injuries. And yes some are almost "R" rated. Humorous and informative, this book gives you an inside look at Ergonomics in places like you've never imagined (i.e. "Gentlemen's Club"). It also provides highlights of a science that takes away people's pain and improves lifestyles. If you've laughed at Dirty Jobs, you'll laugh at Ergonomics of the Absurd. Also included is an extensive catalog of Things Ergonomic which in actuality are ***NOT***. Revealed as sleazy marketing, these include Ergonomic Toilet Seats, Ergonomic Potato Chips and Ergonomic Bricks. Enter the world of Ergonomics of the Absurd with an open mind. You'll enjoy the trip!!–Available on Amazon.com

Other Books & Gifts

Coming Soon

Body Basics–on Amazon.com

Resilience–on Kindle ebook

BYTR Gifts and Souvenirs
also Soon Available

BYTR FYTR pins $2

BYTR Wind-up Clicking Walking Teeth $5

BYTR Temporary Tattoos $2

Executive Gift $18
The World's Best Ergonomic Tool Ever

Check the BYTR Blog for availability

Coming Soon!

The Tightwad's Guide to Designing a Real Ergonomic Computer Workstation

Ways to Address Injury and Pain from Intensive Computer Usage by developing an ergonomic workstation on little or no budget

Short on cash? Long on pain, numbness and tingling? Having difficulty finishing your professional work product…or that game?

Got the need and desire, but not the funds to do a computer workstation makeover?

You can't make any money if you are in pain. It's hard to get out of pain if you don't have any money.

Help is Here!

Answers & solutions allow you to care for your health with a tightwad budget.

Check the BYTR Blog for launch date

www.ingramcontent.com/pod-product-compliance
Lightning Source LLC
Chambersburg PA
CBHW052139070326
40690CB00047B/1098

9781717428592